HEALTH AND FITNESS
PROFESSIONALS

PRACTICAL CAREER GUIDES

Series Editor: Kezia Endsley

Dental Assistants and Hygienists, by Kezia Endsley
Health and Fitness Professionals, by Kezia Endsley
Medical Office Professionals, by Marcia Santore

HEALTH AND FITNESS PROFESSIONALS

A Practical Career Guide

KEZIA ENDSLEY

ROWMAN & LITTLEFIELD
Lanham • Boulder • New York • London

Published by Rowman & Littlefield
An imprint of The Rowman & Littlefield Publishing Group, Inc.
4501 Forbes Boulevard, Suite 200, Lanham, Maryland 20706
www.rowman.com

Unit A, Whitacre Mews, 26-34 Stannary Street, London SE11 4AB

British Library Cataloguing in Publication Information Available

Library of Congress Cataloging-in-Publication Data

Names: Endsley, Kezia, 1968– author.
Title: Health and fitness professionals : practical career guide / Kezia Endsley.
Description: Lanham : Rowman & Littlefield, 2019. | Includes bibliographical references.
Identifiers: LCCN 2018032781 (print) | LCCN 2018033551 (ebook) |
    ISBN 9781538111840 (electronic) | ISBN 9781538111833 (paperback : alk. paper)
Subjects: LCSH: Allied health personnel—Vocational guidance.
Classification: LCC R697.A4 (ebook) | LCC R697.A4 E53 2019 (print) |
    DDC 610.73/7069—dc23
LC record available at https://lccn.loc.gov/2018032781

Printed in the United States of America

To Piper,
who is getting ready for her journey.
You make me so proud.

Contents

Acknowledgments

Thanks always go to my stalwart husband, Erik, who holds down the fort regardless of the hurricanes that come through, rocking the foundation. A special thanks also to Jeff Busha for all his help and support in finding contacts for the interviews in this book.

Introduction: The Allied Health Professions

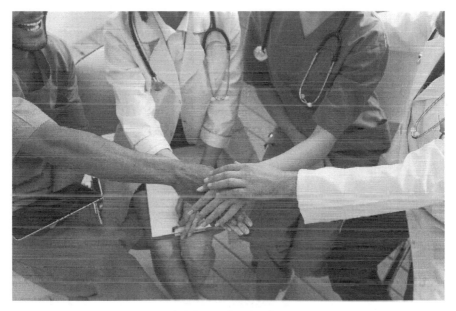

In it to save lives together

*W*elcome to the allied health professions! If you are interested in a career in the health and fitness field (the allied health field, as it is often called), you've come to the right book. These are professions that are related to, but don't include, nursing, medicine, dentistry, or pharmacy. They serve as allies in health and fitness and often work in healthcare teams to the benefit of their patients. They provide services pertaining to the diagnosis, evaluation, and prevention of diseases and disorders; fitness regimens to address or prevent illness and injury; dietary and nutrition services; rehabilitation and health systems management; among others.

There is a lot of good news about this field, and it's a very smart career choice for anyone with a passion to help people improve their physical health and fitness. It's a great career for people who get energy from working with other people and want to help others live their fullest lives. Job demand is high and there continues to be a shortage of people entering the workforce in all these areas.

When considering any career, your goal should be to find your specific nexus of interest, talent, passion, and job demand. Yes, it is important to consider job outlook and demand, educational requirements, and other such practical matters, but remember that you'll be spending a large portion of your life in whatever career you choose, so you should also find something that you enjoy doing and are passionate about. Of course, it can make the road easier to walk if you choose something that's in demand and lucrative. That's where the various health and fitness professions shine!

A Career in Allied Health

This book covers six main areas of health and fitness that have proven to be stable, lucrative, and growing professions. These are:

- Physical therapy
- Occupational therapy
- Recreational therapy
- Exercise physiology
- Massage therapy
- Athletic training

(Did you know that as many as one hundred different professions fall under the umbrella of allied health? As a matter of practicality, only these six are covered here, based in part on the healthy demand for practitioners in these six particular areas. Other professions in the allied health area include dental assistants and hygienists, chiropractors, speech therapists, nutritionists, emergency medical technicians and paramedics, and medical assistants. There are even more than are listed here. Check out the US Bureau of Labor Statistics website at https://www.bls.gov/ooh/healthcare/home.htm for an example of other professions under this umbrella.)

So what exactly do these people do on the job, day in and day out? What skills and educational background do you need to succeed in these professions? How much can you expect to make, and what are the pros and cons of these various professions? Do these careers have a bright future? Is this even the right career path for you? How do you avoid burnout and deal with stress? This book can help you answer these questions and more.

> "I am often surprised by how much I love it [being an occupational therapist] and how passionate I am—it's become a part of me. It influences and informs how I function in my life."—Laura Isaacs, OTR

For each of these six professions, the book covers the pros and cons, educational requirements, projected annual wages, personality traits that are well suited, working conditions and expectations, and more. You'll even read some interviews from real professionals working in these industries. The goal is for you to learn enough about these professions to give you a clear view as to which one, if any, is a good fit for you. And if you still have more questions, this book will also point you to resources where you can learn even more.

An important note: Regardless of the career you might choose under the allied health umbrella, you need to have a lifelong curiosity and love of learning. Your education won't be over once you finish your degree or training. In fact, maintaining current certifications and meeting or exceeding continuing education requirements (usually set forth by the governing board and/or by state regulations where you practice) is all very important in the allied health careers.

The Market Today

The good news is that the US Bureau of Labor Statistics forecasts that healthcare in general will be the fastest growing field in the decade between the years 2016 and 2026.[1] (See https://www.bls.gov/emp/ for a full list of employment projections.) This field includes the allied health professions. Not only does this translate into job security, but it also means that more new positions are being created within the healthcare and fitness industries every year.

The demand for practitioners in allied health continue to grow in the United States due to many factors:

- We have a large elderly population, as the generation of baby boomers continues to age. This elderly population struggles with chronic conditions that affect mobility, such as diabetes and obesity.
- Other growing diseases, disorders, and illnesses—including Alzheimer's disease, cerebral palsy, attention deficit hyperactivity disorder (ADHD), and autism—demand continuing services.
- Hospitals and healthcare professionals are emphasizing exercise and preventive care to help patients recover from cardiovascular and pulmonary diseases and improve their overall health.
- Treatments in injury prevention and detection continue to evolve and become more complicated.
- Increasing information and expectations from the public about injury treatment and prevention translate to higher demand for care.
- A decrease in the number of primary care physicians and stricter cost-control measures lead to greater demand for health-related treatments.
- Children and young adults continue to participate more competitively in sports at younger ages, which leads to more sports-related injuries and illnesses.

Chapter 1 covers lots more about the job prospects of all these professions, breaking down the numbers for each one in more detail.

What Does This Book Cover?

The goal of this book is to cover all aspects of your search for an allied health degree and explain how the professions work and how you can excel in them. Here's a breakdown of the chapters:

- Chapter 1 explains the six different careers under the health and fitness umbrella covered in this book: physical therapy, occupational therapy, recreational therapy, exercise physiology, massage therapy, and athletic training. You'll learn about what people in these professions do in their day-to-day work, the environments where you can find these people working, some pros and cons about each career path, the average salaries of these jobs, and the outlook in the future for all these careers.

- Chapter 2 explains in detail the educational requirements of these six different careers, from postsecondary certificates to doctoral degrees. You will learn how to go about getting experience (in the form of shadowing, internships, and fieldwork) in these professions before you enter college as well as during your college years.

- Chapter 3 explains all the aspects of college and postsecondary schooling that you'll want to consider as you move forward. You will learn about the great schools out there and how to get the best education for the best deal. You will also learn a little about scholarships and financial aid and how the SAT and ACT work.

- Chapter 4 covers all aspects of the résumé-writing and interviewing processes, including writing a stellar résumé and cover letter, interviewing to your best potential, dressing for the part, communicating effectively and efficiently, and more.

Where Do You Start?

The allied health field—and the six professions covered specifically in this book—is so vast and varied that you can approach a career in health and fitness from many angles. Are you more interested in the science and biology behind it all, or do you feel that you would be great at working with and helping people? Do you enjoy being fit and helping athletes be healthy and strong, or would you rather help people with disabilities function at their highest level? Are you better with kids and babies, or do you enjoy working with the elderly?

The good news is that you don't need to know the answers to these questions yet. In order to find the best fit for yourself in the allied health professions, you need to understand how these jobs work. That's where you'll start in chapter 1.

Why Choose a Career in the Health and Fitness Field?

You learned in the introduction that the allied health field, which includes the six professions covered in this book, is large, healthy, and growing. You also learned a little bit about how a career in these professions is different from, yet related to, a career in nursing or medicine. You also were reminded that it's important to pursue a career that you enjoy, are good at, and are passionate about. You will spend a lot of your life working; it makes sense to find something you enjoy doing. Of course, you want to make money and support yourself while doing it. If you love the idea of helping people for a living, you've come to the right book.

This book covers these six health and fitness professions:

- Physical therapy
- Occupational therapy
- Recreational therapy
- Exercise physiology
- Massage therapy
- Athletic training

This chapter breaks out these six professions and covers the basics of each. The nice thing is that no matter what degree of postsecondary education you can or want to pursue, there is a way for you to choose an allied health profession and be a part of the health and fitness world. After reading this chapter, you should have a good understanding of each career and can then start to determine if one of them is a good fit for you. Let's start with physical therapy.

What Is Physical Therapy?

Physical therapy is the process of using actual movements (sometimes called biomechanics or kinesiology), exercise therapy, and manual (hands-on) therapy to manipulate and move soft tissue and joints in order to improve a person's physical impairment and reduce any related pain. These treatments can include massage, hydrotherapy (using water), and manual stimulation, but not the use of medicines, surgery, or radiation.[1]

The goal is to generally increase the person's mobility and restore function to the impaired area. Impaired function/movement can be the result of many factors, including sports injuries, age, disease, or congenital issues. Physical therapy attempts to improve a person's quality of life through expert examination of physical injuries, proper diagnosis, and effective intervention.

Simply stated, physical therapists (PTs) help injured people improve their movement and manage any pain. These therapists are often an important part of the rehabilitation, treatment, and preventive care of patients with chronic conditions, illnesses, or injuries. People in need of physical therapy who don't seek

Physical therapist helping a young woman

treatment may very well find that their condition worsens over time. PTs often work with a team of professionals, including occupational therapists (OTs), speech therapists, personal physicians, and more. They treat patients with hands-on, manual therapy and develop a plan of action for recovery and pain reduction.

Modern PTs can choose to work in a variety of settings, including private clinics and offices, nursing homes, hospitals, and even in patient homes.[2] Regardless of the workplace setting, they spend much of their time on their feet, working actively with patients. If you decide to become a PT, it's wise to remain physically fit and healthy yourself.

As a PT, you will become an expert in how the musculoskeletal and neuromuscular systems work. PTs work on muscle-, joint-, and nerve-related issues. PTs entering the profession need a doctor of physical therapy (DPT) degree. You will also be required to be licensed as a PT in the state in which you practice.[3] Chapter 2 covers the educational and professional certification requirements in more detail.

A BRIEF HISTORY OF PHYSICAL THERAPY

The field of physical therapy developed in the United States during World War I in an effort to treat soldiers' injuries as a result of the war. When polio hit the United States severely between 1920 and 1940, this led to many people—young and old alike—developing motor paralysis, which, it turned out, could be helped with physical therapy.[4] It was in 1921 that the first professional organization for PTs, called the American Women's Physical Therapeutic Association, was formed. This later changed its name to the American Physical Therapy Association (APTA). World War II also contributed to the advancement of this field, as advances in medicine meant that more wounded soldiers survived their injuries and needed physical therapy. The field of physical therapy continued to evolve and grow as soldiers from later wars needed care and treatment.

Today, the profession of physical therapy has evolved to treat not only multiple types of diverse injuries, but also to prevent impairments associated with certain disease processes. The profession of physical therapy is now international, and outside of the United States, the profession is called physiotherapy and PTs are called physiotherapists.[5]

THE PROS AND CONS OF PHYSICAL THERAPY

The field of physical therapy is healthy and growing, as you'll learn later in this chapter. If you choose to become a PT, you'll enjoy a lucrative salary and job security. In addition to security, the PT profession affords flexible work hours and is a profession that you can practice part-time without negative ramifications. Because it's practiced in many different settings, the day-to-day environment can vary greatly, which means you can find the kind of workplace that matches your needs and personality without leaving your profession. Maybe the greatest pro associated with this career is that you'll also be able to help people live fuller lives, free (or nearly free) of pain.

Despite its many advantages, there are a few cons to consider as well. One rather large hurdle to consider is the need to have a DPT degree, which typically requires an additional three years of study after you receive your undergraduate degree. Although PTs in the past could practice with a master's degree, all current students must now successfully complete the DPT degree to become practicing PTs. Another issue to keep in mind is the physicality of the job. You will be on your feet and working hands-on with your patients all day. Ironically, this can lead to chronic physical issues, such as back pain, that you need to be ready to manage and treat yourself.

As with all healthcare professions, there is always a risk of infection when working around patient populations, especially if you work in a hospital, nursing home, or healthcare facility.

HOW HEALTHY IS THE PT JOB MARKET?

The Bureau of Labor Statistics (BLS) is part of the US Department of Labor. It tracks statistical information about thousands of careers in the United States. For anyone studying to become a PT, the news is great! Employment is expected to grow 28 percent in the decade from 2016 to 2026, which is much faster than the average. PTs are expected to be in great demand as the generation of baby boomers continues to age and our population continues to struggle with chronic conditions that affect mobility, such as diabetes and obesity.

These statistics show just how promising this career is now and in the foreseeable future:

- *Education*: Doctoral degree (doctor of physical therapy); licensing re-quired in all states
- *2016 median pay:* $85,400
- *Job outlook 2016–2026:* 28 percent (much faster than average)
- *Work environment:* Mainly office (34 percent) or hospital (27 percent) settings, with smaller numbers working in home healthcare and nursing home settings (15 percent)[6]

The jury is in: Physical therapy is a promising and lucrative career!

RUNNING A PRIVATE PHYSICAL THERAPY PRACTICE

Jeff Busha

Jeff Busha, PT, MBA, MS, COMT, OCS, opened his physical therapy practice in 2004 with his wife, also a PT. He began his career working in patient care as a therapist in several hospital settings. He then moved to a large practice as a partner before beginning his own private practice. His specialty is musculoskel-etal orthopedic medicine.

What is a typical day in your job?

Since it's just my wife and me running our small practice, my days are long— usually 7:00 a.m. to 6:00 p.m.—and filled with patient care. I see patients every half hour. We treat with manual therapy and then develop a plan of action, with instructions to our patients about what kind of exercise they should do at home to continue treatment. Our typical cases include spinal injuries, neck issues such as pinched nerves, and back issues such as disk problems. All our issues are muscle, joint, and nerve related. Any business-related issues have to wait until after normal work hours.

What's the best part of your job?

I enjoy being able to treat the unusual and hard-to-treat cases. Patients come in frustrated and discouraged because they have been to other therapists and nothing has worked. In many cases, we can get to the root of the problem and help them heal. It's rewarding to be able to help them! One example is chronic myofascial pain, where manual therapy works well. Patients are often frustrated and it's very rewarding to help them.

Myofascial pain syndrome is a disorder whereby pressure on sensitive points in the muscles causes pain in what seem like unrelated body parts. This sometimes happens after recurring injuries or muscle overuse. Symptoms include chronic pain or a tender muscle knot.

The best thing about private practice is the freedom to treat people how you want to treat them. There are no limitations like you might have at a hospital, and no productivity requirements like you might have at a large PT practice. I really get to do what's best for the patient—schedule them for longer if needed, for example—and my patients do appreciate that.

What's the worst part of your job?

Charting and dealing with insurance. It's more and more demanding and there are more hoops to jump through to justify to insurance that treatment is necessary. More paperwork and screening procedures are necessary than even before. We do most of the charting at the end of the day or after normal hours, which can make the days long at times.

What's the most surprising thing about your job?

You learn something every day from your patients. You sometimes don't have the answers, which is not what you learn in school or what the medical community sometimes wants to admit. Listening to your patients is a good way to learn. Keep an open mind and you'll continue to learn.

What's next? Where do you see yourself going from here?

I am happy where I am at. I enjoy the freedom I get from my private practice. Maybe I will teach continuing education to other PTs. Maybe teach in a PT school setting, as I have done that in the past and enjoyed it.

Did your education prepare you for the job?

Yes, I really think it did. Graduating from PT school leaves you competent to treat people. Continuing education and board certifications are very important as well, as they will help you treat people at an advanced level as your career progresses.

Is the job what you expected?

Yes, although I didn't know that I would end up with my own practice. I started off pursuing an electrical engineer degree, but found that I loved the science portion of my education the best. Volunteering at a PT clinic in the summer during college in my town in Michigan sparked my interest, and the rest, as they say, is history!

Since you own your own business, how do you acquire your clients?

On the one hand, physicians typically refer patients to us. Also, people come in based on word of mouth from friends and families, or even from seeing us online. It's probably fifty-fifty word of mouth and physician referrals. Having your own practice is getting harder these days, as most physicians have to refer in-house, but I have been successful in growing my practice and am very grateful for it.

Any advice for young people thinking about going into this field?

It's important to keep in mind that the field is very competitive. You need at least a 3.8 GPA to even be considered. You must also be able to interview well and be [a] good communicator, which shows you can deal with patients well. You must keep your grades up and have some hours of volunteer work to stand out from the crowd.

It's a good idea to seek out volunteer work and get exposed to various aspects of physical therapy so you know what they are all like. Each area—hospital, private practice, sports medicine, pediatrics, women's health, neurologically impaired, etc.—has its pros and cons. In your last year in the program, you work clinic rotations full-time, which also helps in determining which area you might like to concentrate on.

Something to keep in mind is that patients sometimes plateau—say, they get to about 70 or 80 percent better—and then that's all you can do for them. They have to manage the rest through exercise. You have to be ready to accept that you can't cure everyone all the time. Sometimes people will need surgery; that's the bottom line.

The good news is that the large baby boomer generation [will need a] PT as they continue to age, so there is still a very strong demand. You won't have an issue getting a job. It's also a good job for part-timers and provides work flexibility, so it's easier to have some kind of work-life balance.

================

WHAT IS A PHYSICAL THERAPIST ASSISTANT?

Physical therapist assistants (PTAs) work with and under the supervision and direction of licensed PTs. They work in medical offices and hospitals performing the same types of therapy that a PT performs. According to the BLS, this job is currently growing at 30 percent, which is much faster than the national average. The mean pay in the United States is $45,290. PTAs entering the profession only need an associate's degree from an accredited program (usually a two-year degree), rather than a doctoral degree. This can be a more economical (albeit slower) way to work toward a PT degree, as you could use your PTA experience and on-the-job training to later enter PT school, all the while earning a living. Check out www.apta.org/PTACareers/Overview/ for more information.

AM I RIGHT FOR PHYSICAL THERAPY?

Ask yourself these questions:

- Do I mind touching people I don't know, or could I learn to be comfortable with this idea?
- Am I comfortable around people who are sick or disabled?
- Do I like meeting, talking with, and helping people?
- Am I ready to spend most of my working day on my feet?
- Am I ready to spend up to seven additional years in school after high school pursuing a doctoral degree?
- Am I a lifelong learner and excited at the prospect of continuously learning about new research related to my profession?

- Am I ready to give advice that might not be followed even if it's best for my clients? Can I accept that not everyone will do what's best for them?

If the answer to any of these questions is an adamant *no*, you might want to consider a different path. Fortunately, there are myriad healthcare and fitness options, five more of which are covered in this very book!

What Is Occupational Therapy?

Occupational therapy is a specialized form of therapy for people recuperating from or managing physical or mental illnesses, with the goal to help people best perform their daily "occupations," whether that be a student, a retiree, a baby, or other. Rehabilitation focuses on helping people perform and master activities required in their daily life.[7] In simplest terms, OTs help people participate in the things they want and need to do, the skills needed for daily living and working. This is done through the therapeutic use of everyday activities (occupations).[8]

For example, OTs do things like help children with disabilities participate fully in school and social situations. In a school setting, they might help children with sensory issues cope with the busy classroom environment, help students using wheelchairs manage the classroom and use a desk masterfully, or help other children develop techniques to sit quietly in class for sustained periods.

OTs also provide support to older adults with physical and cognitive changes. In these cases, an OT might help an adult who has suffered a stroke use adaptive equipment to put on his or her shoes, brush his or her teeth, or get out of a chair.

OT intervention typically starts with an evaluation of the person's home and other environments, recommendations for adaptive equipment if necessary, and

---

The OT profession in a nutshell: "Helping people function at their highest level whatever their 'occupation' is. OTs don't help people find jobs, which is what some people think. They focus on helping people get back to living life to the fullest." —Laura Issacs, OTR

guidance and education for family members and caregivers. OTs take a holistic approach, where the focus is on adapting the environment to fit the person.[9]

Just like PTs, OTs work in a variety of settings—including hospitals, schools, clinics, nursing facilities, community centers, healthcare facilities, and patient homes. Also just like PTs, OTs spend a lot of their time on their feet, working actively with patients.

OTs entering the profession need a master of science in occupational therapy (MSOT) degree, which typically takes two additional years after completing an undergraduate degree. All states require OTs to become licensed. To earn your license, you'll need a degree from an accredited program and your National Board for Certification in Occupational Therapy (NBCOT) certification.[10] In addition, there is some talk about moving toward the requirement of a doctoratal degree to be an OT, although that is not the case yet. Chapter 2 covers the educational and professional certification requirements in more detail.

THE PROS AND CONS OF OCCUPATIONAL THERAPY

The field of occupational therapy is healthy and growing, as you'll learn later in this chapter. If you choose to become an OT, you'll enjoy a lucrative salary and job security. If the idea of being a PT appeals to you, but you don't want (or can't afford) to go to school for the entire time required to become PT, occupational therapy may be a more appealing route for you to consider.

Because it's practiced in many different settings, the day-to-day work environment of an OT can vary greatly, which means you can find the kind of workplace and patient type that match your needs and personality without leaving your profession. For example, if you enjoy working with children, you could be an OT for a school district. If you prefer to work with even younger children, perhaps babies, you can serve as an OT in that role as well, helping very young children reach developmental milestones through occupational therapy. Each setting is very different, with a different set of patients and challenges. Perhaps the greatest pro associated with this career is that you'll also be able to help people live fuller lives, based on their own priorities and physical needs.

Despite its many advantages, there are a few cons to consider as well. You are committed to additional study after your undergraduate degree, as well as additional certifications and licensure, which costs time and money. Another issue to keep in mind is the physicality of the job. In many cases, especially when working with the elderly, you will be on your feet and working hands-on with your patients all day. Ironically, this can lead to chronic physical issues, such as back pain, that you need to be ready to manage and treat yourself. This career can also be emotionally challenging as you deal with frustrated patients dealing with diminished physical and cognitive capabilities.

Finally, as with all healthcare professions, there is always a risk of infection when working around patient populations, especially if you work in a hospital, nursing home, or healthcare facility.

HOW HEALTHY IS THE OT JOB MARKET?

The BLS tracks statistical information about thousands of careers in the United States. For anyone studying to become an OT, the news is great! Employment is expected to grow 24 percent in the decade from 2016 to 2026, which is much faster than the average. OTs are expected to be in continued demand due to diseases and illnesses such as Alzheimer's disease, cerebral palsy, autism, and more.

These statistics show just how promising this career is now and in the foreseeable future:

- *Education:* Master's degree; licensing required in all states
- *2016 median pay:* $81,900
- *Job outlook 2016–2026:* 24 percent (much faster than average)
- *Work environment:* Half in offices or hospitals, with smaller numbers working in schools, nursing homes, and home health services[11]

AM I RIGHT FOR OCCUPATIONAL THERAPY?

Ask yourself these questions:

- Do I mind touching people I don't know, or could I learn to be comfortable with this idea?
- Do I like meeting, talking with, and helping people?
- Am I comfortable around people who are sick or disabled?
- Am I ready to be an advocate for my patients?

- Am I ready to spend two additional years in graduate school pursuing a master's degree?
- Can I handle the emotional issues that accompany dealing with people with chronic physical or cognitive issues and the diminished capabilities that come with that?
- Am I ready to give advice that might not be followed even if it's best for my clients? Can I accept that not everyone will do what's best for them?

If the answer to any of these questions is an adamant *no*, you might want to consider a different path. Fortunately, there are myriad healthcare and fitness options, five more of which are covered in this very book!

What Is Recreational Therapy?

Recreational therapy, also known as therapeutic recreation, is a specialized type of therapy that uses recreation—such as games, sports, crafts, dance, music, work with animals, and more—to help people with illnesses or disabilities recover, maintain well-being, or lead a fuller and healthier life.[12] This approach is unique in the techniques and methods used for rehabilitation.

The focus of a recreational therapist (RT) is on physical, mental, and emotional well-being. Recreational therapy focuses on cognitive and physical impairments and can help reduce depression, stress, and anxiety as well as improve basic motor functioning and reasoning abilities. With individualized goals and treatment plans for each person, the goal is to eliminate any activity limitations and restrictions to participating in life through the use of recreational activities.

RTs work in many different settings, including hospitals, school systems, nursing homes, and parks and recreation departments. One area that many RTs find very rewarding is in working with service members—active military and veterans—who have physical and psychological injuries or disorders due to combat. Whatever the setting, the focus is on keeping patients as active, healthy, and independent as possible in their chosen life pursuits. Most therapists work full-time.[13]

RTs typically need a bachelor's degree, but associate's degree tracks are also available. Many employers also require that RTs be certified. Board-certified RTs are called certified therapeutic recreation specialists (CTRSs). To be certified,

Child having a sensory integration session

you must earn a bachelor's degree, complete an internship in the field, and then pass an exam. Chapter 2 covers the educational and professional certification requirements in more detail.

THE PROS AND CONS OF RECREATIONAL THERAPY

The field of recreational therapy is not growing as much as the fields of OT and PT, as you'll learn later in this chapter. It maintains a pace of growth matched with the national average job market. However, if you really want to be a therapist but can't afford to attend graduate school, being an RT is a good option because you simply need a bachelor's degree to practice.

Because it's practiced in many different settings, the day-to-day work environment of an RT can vary greatly, which means you can find the kind of workplace and patient type that match your needs and personality. You could very well spend much of your job outdoors at the park or at the local gym. You will likely spend your work hours around recreational activities, animals, and other such activities. The treatment plans that you develop for your clients can introduce creativity and fun into your job. In addition, you will be helping people live fuller lives and recover from illnesses through the use of fun activities!

As with the other types of therapy, you will be on your feet and working hands-on with your patients all day. This career can also be emotionally challenging as you deal with frustrated patients dealing with diminished physical and cognitive capabilities. In addition, the job market is not as robust as with other careers in similar fields. That means you have to get the grades, experience, and exposure to stand out in a more competitive job market.

Finally, as with all healthcare professions, there is always a risk of infection when working around patient populations, especially if you work in a hospital, nursing home, or healthcare facility.

HOW HEALTHY IS THE RT JOB MARKET?

The BLS tracks statistical information about thousands of careers in the United States. According to BLS statistics, the US job market for a RT is expected to grow 7 percent in the decade from 2016 to 2026, which is on pace with the average job market. RTs are expected to be in continued demand due to the large elderly population. Job prospects look best for RTs who have a bachelor's degree and proper certification, and who specialize in working with the elderly.

These statistics show just how promising this career is now and in the foreseeable future:

- *Education:* Bachelor's degree; licensing required by many employers
- *2016 median pay:* $46,400
- *Job outlook 2016–2026:* 7 percent (as fast as average)
- *Work environment:* Includes parks and recreation departments, hospitals, schools, nursing homes, and home health services[14]

AM I RIGHT FOR RECREATIONAL THERAPY?

Ask yourself these questions:

- Do I like meeting, talking with, and helping people?
- Am I comfortable around people who are sick or disabled?
- Am I ready to spend most of my working day on my feet?

- Can I handle the emotional issues that accompany dealing with people with chronic physical or cognitive issues and the diminished capabilities that come with that?
- Am I willing to do the extra work needed to stand out from the crowd so as to find a good job in a competitive market?

If the answer to any of these questions is an adamant *no*, you might want to consider a different path. Fortunately, there are myriad healthcare and fitness options, five more of which are covered in this very book!

What Is Exercise Physiology?

Exercise physiology is the process of analyzing a person's medical history and current level of fitness in order to develop the best exercise and fitness routine for the individual's needs and health status. Exercise physiologists (EPs) are also involved in implementing exercise plans and guide their clients in the proper approach, form, and schedule.[15] They typically work with patients who have chronic conditions—such as diabetes, lung disease, heart disease, and other cardiovascular impairments—to help them improve their overall health and fitness. Some work closely with primary care doctors who prescribe exercise regimens to their patients as part of their long-term treatment. They also can work with both amateur and professional athletes who want to boost their performance.

EPs differ from athletic trainers in that they are expected to have a wide range of knowledge about the human body and the benefit that exercise has on it, both mentally and physically. EPs are knowledgeable about the effects of exercise on the musculoskeletal system as well as on the cardiovascular and endocrine (hormonal) systems. EPs are healthcare professionals who have completed a degree in exercise physiology. They prescribe a course of action for fitness or rehabilitation.[16]

Some EPs take a different path: research. In fact, much of what we know about the body's responses to various types of physical activity comes from their research. They study a wide range of applied physiology topics, such as muscle composition, cardiorespiratory (heart and lung) capacities, and how energy is used and produced during exercise. EPs are often needed as clinical research assistants in studies involving the physiological effects of exercise. They coordinate sports medicine research studies, which are typically related to exercise and fitness, to determine the effects on the human body. They develop and supervise these clinical trials. In addition, they may work for companies that create supplements and vitamins, for example, in order to define and test the body's response to new macro- and micronutrient formulations.

THE PROS AND CONS OF EXERCISE PHYSIOLOGY

The field of exercise physiology is growing at a rate that's higher than the national average, as you'll learn later in this section. It is still a small occupation in terms of overall employment numbers, which means that competition for available positions will likely remain high. Exercise physiology is more focused on the science—the biology—of the human body, and if you are particularly interested in anatomy, kinesiology, and nutrition, this will be an interesting career for you. Most EPs in the United States are self-employed and hired independently, which has benefits and drawbacks. If you want to run your own business and enjoy the freedom of that approach, exercise physiology is a good option.

Becoming an EP requires no advanced degrees beyond a bachelor's degree. Certification requirements vary by state, but are minimal. However, to increase your job prospects, it's wise to be certified by the American Society of Exercise Physiologists (ASEP).[17]

HOW HEALTHY IS THE EXERCISE PHYSIOLOGY JOB MARKET?

The BLS tracks statistical information about thousands of careers in the United States. According to BLS statistics, the US job market for an EP is expected to grow 13 percent in the decade from 2016 to 2026, which is faster than the average. Demand could rise as hospitals and healthcare professionals continue emphasizing exercise and preventive care to help patients recover from cardiovascular and pulmonary diseases and improve their overall health.

These statistics show just how promising this career is now and in the foreseeable future:

- *Education:* Bachelor's degree; minimal licensing requirements, depending on the state
- *2016 median pay:* $47,340
- *Job outlook 2016–2026:* 13 percent (faster than average)
- *Work environment:* More than half self-employed in 2016; others in hospitals and healthcare providers[18]

AM I RIGHT FOR EXERCISE PHYSIOLOGY?

Ask yourself these questions:

- Do I like meeting, talking with, and helping people?
- Am I comfortable around people who are sick or disabled?
- Am I ready to spend most of my working day on my feet?
- Am I willing to do the extra work needed to stand out from the crowd so as to find a good job in a competitive market?
- Do I enjoy learning about the biology of the human body and exercise science specifically?

If the answer to any of these questions is an adamant *no*, you might want to consider a different path. However, if you find yourself pursuing the clinical research route of exercise physiology, you won't likely work with patients and others on a daily basis, and your job could be a lot less physically taxing. In this case, you'll be managing a clinical trial with other healthcare officials, such as doctors and clinical scientists. This might be a better fit if you are not comfortable working with the patient population on a daily basis.

What Is Massage Therapy?

Massage therapy involves treating clients' physical ailments using touch to manipulate muscles and other soft tissues of the body. Massage therapists use touch to alleviate pain, help heal injuries, improve circulation, relieve stress, increase relaxation, and aid in the general wellness of their clients.[19] In addition to performing massage therapy, massage therapists are often asked to evaluate clients and determine local painful or tense areas and to provide guidance to clients about proper stretching and relaxation routines. They often develop personalized treatment plans with their long-term clients.

Massage therapists often specialize in one or several different types of massage (known as modalities). These include deep-tissue massage, Swedish massage, infant massage, clinical massage, and prenatal massage, for example. These modalities all require different techniques be applied to the process of massage. The type of massage given typically depends on the client's needs and physical condition, which is up to the massage therapist to recommend along with the client's needs and desires.

THE PROS AND CONS OF MASSAGE THERAPY

The field of massage therapy is healthy and growing much faster than the average, as you'll learn later in this chapter. If you choose to become a massage therapist, you'll enjoy job security and a flexible schedule that can promote a work-life balance.

The benefits to being a massage therapist are many. After meeting relatively short educational requirements (about 500–750 hours of schooling/clinicals, although this depends on the state), you can begin practicing. You don't need a bachelor's degree to practice, but, as with many professions, it's smart (and often required, depending on the state) to pursue continuing education each year, perhaps by learning a new modality, for example.

The job also provides a lot of flexibility in terms of hours and the kinds of patients you choose to see. In addition, you are responsible for helping people feel better and heal, and sometimes those results can even be seen immediately. Another great advantage is that there are many different environments you can choose to work in, including spa settings, medical offices/hospitals, corporate massage settings, gyms, private practice, mobile massages, parties, events, cruise ships and vacation spots, and more. The setting you choose also affects the kind of clientele you will be seeing.

Massage therapy, perhaps more than any other profession discussed in this chapter, is physically demanding. Because of the manual, physical pressure you place on your own muscles and joints, it's important to take care of yourself both physically and mentally. (Yes, massage therapists regularly get massages!) Building a lucrative and consistent base of clients can also take a lot of networking and time, so you may not start out making very much money. You can shorten this journey by being knowledgeable in multiple modalities and by working in environments that help you build from a solid base of existing clients, such as a spa or gym setting.

Massage therapy is also generally considered a high-burnout job, as it's often seen as physically and emotionally draining. The pay isn't stellar and the hours can be difficult, but with hard work and effort, you can make a decent living doing it.

HOW HEALTHY IS THE MASSAGE THERAPY JOB MARKET?

The BLS tracks statistical information about thousands of careers in the United States. For anyone studying to become a massage therapist, the news is great! Employment is expected to grow 26 percent in the decade from 2016 to 2026, which is much faster than the average. Being certified and passing professional exams will better your job prospects, as will being knowledgeable in multiple modalities of massage. When you are new at massage therapy, it does take some time to build your client base.

These statistics show just how reliable this career is now and in the foreseeable future:

- *Education:* Postsecondary nondegree award
- *2016 median pay:* $39,860
- *Job outlook 2016–2026:* 26 percent (much faster than average)
- *Work environment:* Includes spas, franchised clinics, doctor offices, hotels, fitness centers, and private residences[20]

ORIGINS OF MASSAGE THERAPY

Of all the careers covered in this book, massage therapy is arguably the oldest. The first written records mentioning massage therapy date back to 2700 BCE in China and Egypt. Records written in the ancient Indian language Sanskrit indicate that massage was practiced in India long before the beginning of recorded history.[21] Many drawings and paintings in tombs and temples show people receiving massages as well. It's clear that humans have known about the healing power of touch for many centuries now.

AM I RIGHT FOR MASSAGE THERAPY?

Ask yourself these questions:

- Do I mind touching people I don't know, or could I learn to be comfortable with this idea?
- Am I comfortable with the naked body?
- Do I like meeting, talking with, and helping people?
- Am I ready to spend most of my working day on my feet?
- Am I comfortable networking with people and/or marketing myself to build my client base?
- Am I comfortable being alone in a room with all kinds of people?
- Am I able to easily let go of others' worries and burdens?

If the answer to any of these questions is an adamant *no*, you might want to consider a different path. Fortunately, there are myriad healthcare and fitness options, five more of which are covered in this very book!

What Is Athletic Training?

Athletic trainers overwhelmingly work in educational settings—such as high schools, colleges, and universities—under the direction of an athletic department or a specific sports team. They specialize in preventing, diagnosing, and treating muscle and bone injuries and illnesses that occur due to athletic activities. This can be done through developing and enacting proper conditioning and training regimens as well as providing first aid, acute care, and rehabilitation to players.[22] In a very real sense, it's where sports and medicine meet.

Athletic trainers often work with a specific sports team, and in that case might travel nights and weekends with that team to games. They also can work in offices and hospitals. They are usually one of the first healthcare providers on the scene when injuries occur on the field.[23] Their job is to recognize and evaluate injuries at the site and perhaps even provide first aid and emergency care. They also often make appropriate referrals to physicians.

Many trainers work under the direction of a licensed physician and with other healthcare providers, often covering specific injuries and treatment options or evaluating and treating patients as directed by a physician. Some meet

Athletic trainer helping an injured runner

with a team physician or consulting physician regularly. In this case, they are considered part of the sports medicine team. As part of that team, they usually coordinate required annual athletic physicals and supervise the clearance of injured athletes before and during sport seasons.

To become a certified athletic trainer (ATC), you need a bachelor's or master's degree from an accredited education program and must pass a test administered by the National Athletic Trainers' Association (NATA) as well as state licensure exams. According to the NATA, more than 70 percent of ATCs have a master's or a doctoral degree.

THE PROS AND CONS OF ATHLETIC TRAINING

The field of athletic training is healthy and growing, as you'll learn later in this chapter. If you choose to become an athletic trainer, you'll enjoy a good salary and job security. If you enjoy helping people and love to be involved with and around sports, this is a good career for you. You will help treat injuries, but you can also help develop training regimens to prevent injuries and promote overall health of the athletes, which involves independence and creativity. An important aspect of this job is education, in the sense that you are always promoting methods for injury prevention. The job prospects are strong and will remain so in the near future as well.

> "Make sure you are living the lifestyle that you're promoting."—Sharon Phillips, trainer

Disadvantages include a high stress level in some cases. This work can be stressful, as clients are often in pain and distress and they are looking to you for help. The pressure to win in sports can also be an influence in this career, and you have to be able to balance this with what's right for your athletes. Athletic trainers are often required to work long days, sometimes up to sixty hours a week, and much of that might be administrative tasks such as writing reports, keeping records, and attending meetings. Also, many jobs in this career require at least a master's degree in order to be considered. In fact, if you want to be competitive in this market, you essentially need a master's degree.

HOW HEALTHY IS THE ATHLETIC TRAINING JOB MARKET?

The BLS tracks statistical information about thousands of careers in the United States. For anyone studying to become an athletic trainer, the news is good. Employment is expected to grow 23 percent in the decade from 2016 to 2026, which is much faster than the average. As children and young adults continue to compete at younger ages and more competitively early on in all sorts of sports, this career will continue to have strong growth. Treatments in injury prevention and detection, including the issues surrounding preventing and diagnosing concussions, continue to evolve and be more involved, which means athletic trainers are needed more than before.

These statistics show just how reliable this career is now and in the foreseeable future:

- *Education:* Bachelor's degree, officially, but master's degree becoming the norm in most cases
- *2016 median pay:* $45,630

- *Job outlook 2016–2026:* 23 percent (much faster than average)
- *Work environment:* Mainly educational settings, with medical offices, hospitals, and recreational sports centers a distant second[24]

AM I RIGHT FOR ATHLETIC TRAINING?

Ask yourself these questions:

- Do I like meeting, talking with, and helping people?
- Am I ready to handle emergency situations?
- Am I willing to stay very fit to set an example for my clients?
- Am I ready to spend most of my working day on my feet?
- Do I enjoy being around sports and athletic activities?

If the answer to any of these questions is an adamant *no,* you might want to consider a different path. Fortunately, there are myriad healthcare and fitness options, five more of which are covered in this very book!

CHARACTERISTICS OF SUCCESS IN ALLIED HEALTH FIELDS

Regardless of the profession you choose in allied health, there are commonalities that all people who enjoy success in these areas share. Consider how well the following phrases describe who you are:

- Enjoy helping people
- Enjoy cooperative and collaborative work
- Feel comfortable working with the human body
- Feel comfortable motivating others
- Empathetic toward pain and suffering
- Get energy from being around others
- Interested in biology, kinesiology, and the musculoskeletal system of the human body

If you pursue a career that fundamentally conflicts with the person you are, you won't be good at it and you won't be happy. Don't make that mistake. If you need help in determining your key personality factors, you can take a career counseling questionnaire to find out more. You can find many online or ask you school guidance counselor for reputable sources.

Summary

In this chapter, you learned a lot about six different careers in the health and fitness umbrella—physical therapy, occupational therapy, recreational therapy, exercise physiology, massage therapy, and athletic training. You've learned about what people in these professions do in their day-to-day work, the environments where you can find these people working, some pros and cons about each career path, the average salaries of these jobs, and the outlook in the future for all these careers. You hopefully even contemplated some questions about whether your personal likes and preferences meld well with these jobs. At this time, you should have a good idea what each job looks like. Are you starting to get excited about one field over another? If not, that's okay, as there's still time.

An important takeaway from this chapter is that no matter which of these professions you might pursue, keep in mind that maintaining current certifications and meeting continuing education requirements is very important in all allied health careers. Advances in understanding in the fields of medicine, kinesiology, nutrition, and more are continuous, and it's vitally important that you keep apprised of what's happening if your field. You need to have a lifelong love of learning to succeed in any allied health career.

Chapter 2 dives into forming a plan for your future, covering everything there is to know about educational requirements, certifications, internship and clinical requirements, and more, about each of these careers. You'll learn about finding summer jobs and making the most of volunteer work as well. The goal is for you to set yourself apart—and above—the rest.

2

Forming a Career Plan

Now that you have some idea which career you want to find out more about—or maybe you even know which one you will start pursuing—it's time to formulate a career plan. For you organized folks out there, this can be a helpful and energizing process. If you're not a naturally organized person, or if the idea of looking ahead and building a plan to adulthood scares you, you are not alone. That's what this chapter is for.

After discussing ways to develop a career plan—there is more than one way to do this!—the chapter dives into the various educational requirements of these six professions. Finally, it looks at how you can gain experience through internships, volunteering, clinic work, shadowing, and more. Yes, experience will look good on your résumé, and in some cases it's even required, but even more important, getting out there and experiencing a job in various settings is the best way to determine whether it's really something that you will enjoy. When you find a career that you truly enjoy, it will rarely feel like work at all.

If you still aren't sure which of these professions, if any, is right for you, try a self-assessment questionnaire or a career aptitude test. There are many good ones on the web. As an example, the career resource website Monster.com includes free self-assessment tools at www.monster.com/career-advice/article/best-free-career-assessment-tools. The Princeton Review also has a very good aptitude test geared toward high schoolers at www.princetonreview.com/quiz/career-quiz.

Your ultimate goal should be to match your personal interests and goals with your preparation plan for college and career. Practice articulating your plans and goals to others. When you feel comfortable doing this, that means you have a good grasp of your goals and your plan to reach them.

Planning the Plan

You are on a fact-finding mission of sorts. A career fact-finding plan, no matter what the field, should include these main steps:

- Take some time to consider and jot down your interests and personality traits. Are you a people person, or do you get energy from being alone? Are you creative or analytical? Are you outgoing or shy? Are you organized or creative—or a little of both? Take a career counseling questionnaire (found online or in your guidance counselor's office) to find out more. Consider whether your personal likes and preferences meld well with the jobs you are considering.
- Find out as much as you can about the day-to-day of the job. In what kinds of environments is it performed? Who will you work with? How demanding is the job? What are the challenges? Chapter 1 of this book is designed to help you in this regard.
- Find out about educational requirements and schooling expectations. Will you be able to meet any rigorous requirements? This chapter will help you understand the educational paths of these six professions.
- Seek out opportunities to volunteer or shadow professionals doing the job. Use your critical thinking skills to ask questions and consider whether this is the right environment for you. This chapter also discusses ways to find internships, summer jobs, and other job-related experiences.
- Look into student aid, grants, scholarships, and other ways you can get help to pay for schooling. It's not just about student aid and scholarships, either. Some larger organizations will pay employees to go back to school to get further degrees.
- Build a timetable for taking requirements exams such as the SAT and ACT, applying to schools, visiting schools, and making your decision. You should write down all important deadlines and have them at the ready when you need them.
- Continue to look for employment that matters during your college years—internships and work experiences that help you get hands-on experience in and knowledge about your intended career.

- Find a mentor who is currently practicing in your field of interest. This person can be a great source of information, education, and connections. Don't expect a job (at least not at first); just build a relationship with someone who wants to pass along his or her wisdom and experience. Coffee meetings or even e-mails are a great way to start.

> "Find a good mentor and pick their brain. I had two excellent ones, both of whom really helped further my career."—Jeff Thomas, athletic trainer

Where to Go for Help

If you're aren't sure where to start, your local library, school library, and guidance counselor's office are great places to begin. Search your local or school library for resources about finding a career path and finding the right schooling that fits your needs and budget. Make an appointment with or e-mail a counselor to ask about taking career interest questionnaires. With a little prodding, you'll be directed to lots of good information online and elsewhere. You can start your research with these four sites:

- The Bureau of Labor Statistics (BLS) Career Outlook site at www .bls.gov/careeroutlook/home.htm. The United States Department of Labor's BLS site doesn't just track job statistics, as you learned in chapter 1. An entire section of the BLS website is dedicated to helping young adults looking to uncover their interests to match those interests with jobs currently in the market. Check out the section called "Career Planning for High Schoolers." Information is updated based on career trends and jobs in demand, so you'll get practical information as well.
- The Mapping Your Future site at www.mappingyourfuture.org helps you determine a career path and then helps you map out a plan to reach those goals. It includes tips on preparing for college, paying for college, job hunting, résumé writing, and more.

- The Education Planner site at www.educationplanner.org has separate sections for students, parents, and counselors. It breaks down the task of planning your career goals into simple, easy-to-understand steps. You can find personality assessments, get tips on preparing for school, learn from some Q&As from counselors, download and use a planner worksheet, read about how to finance your education, and more.
- The TeenLife site at www.teenlife.com. Calling itself "the leading source for college preparation," this site includes lots of information about summer programs, gap year programs, community service, and more. Promoting the belief that spending time out "in the world" outside of the classroom can help students do better in school, find a better fit in terms of career, and even interview better with colleges, this site contains lots of links to volunteer and summer programs.

Use these sites as jumping-off points and don't be afraid to reach out to a real person, such as a guidance counselor, if you're feeling overwhelmed.

BEING AN OT MEANS HAVING PASSION FOR THE UNDERDOG!

Laura J. Isaacs

Laura J. Isaacs, occupational therapist registered (OTR), has been a practicing occupational therapist (OT) for twenty years. She began her career working with the elderly in a long-term care setting. She then worked with babies and very young children, evaluating, screening, and treating them for the purposes of early intervention. Since 2009, she has been employed by a school corporation and serves a large population of school-aged children.

Why did you choose to become an OT?

I was originally interested either in medicine or physical therapy, but really didn't have a solid plan as I entered college. My mom kept telling me to look into occupational therapy, but I had some misconceptions about what exactly they did, thinking it was mostly just "crafts" with patients. I then attended an allied health open house at my university and immediately loved the OT part. I realized then that the focus was on helping people get back to life and living life to the fullest. I could see it was a lot of different modalities, and the more I learned, the more interested I became.

You have worked as an OT in lots of different settings. Can you describe your experiences a bit and compare and contrast them?

I worked in long-term care and rehab centers for six years. In that environment, I was working mainly with adults with physical disabilities. I got my first job while in college, working with older people. I helped people who had suffered strokes, broken hips, and other physical impairments related to age or injury. Some of it was acute rehab, where I helped them gain strength and abilities so they could go home. The "occupation" in this case for these adults was to live in their homes, perhaps go back to work, and to function well on their own. Others lived in the long-term care area and so I helped them be stronger so they could do daily activities in the center. That included teaching them how to use adaptive equipment to facilitate daily activities.

After six years working with adults and the elderly, I moved to working with babies and children, ages newborn to three years. I worked for Indiana's early intervention program (First Steps). I helped children meet their developmental milestones. Needs I addressed included play skills, eating, sleeping, and being calm, and of course meeting developmental milestones. Many (although not all) of my patients were either born prematurely or were adopted from other countries and hadn't received adequate stimulation when they were infants. A child's occupation is playing, eating, and sleeping, so I helped them in those areas. I used a lot of toys to build play skills and help them get better (such as teach them how to use both hands together). Another important component of this job was educating families and caregivers to continue therapy at home. You must be able to work alongside the parent or caregiver in the child's home.

I also worked for an outpatient pediatric clinic for a time. This involved more intensive medical-based therapy, sensory integration (ADHD, spectrum, sensory issues, and processing issues). I worked with a core group of OTs, physical therapists (PTs), and speech therapists. This was a very nice setting to do more intensive, medical-based therapy with the kids. Treatment often involved sensory integration, as an example.

What is your typical day working for a school corporation?

I currently work for a special education cooperative that serves seven smaller school systems. They are small and need to share these types of resources (including PT, OT, psychological, and a host of specialized teachers). I am responsible for three different school corporations and see kids from preschool to high school age who have been placed in special education. In this case, the patient's "occupation" is being a student. So this includes therapy addressing behavior management. This can include things like working on tying shoes, getting a coat on, packing up their belongings, working on handwriting, or sitting still in classroom. I work closely with teachers in developing a behavior management plan.

I have a list of students that I see, and I set my own schedule in terms of when I see them within a week or month. I see kids in the classroom or sometimes pull them out (you want to be least disruptive to the learning environment as possible). I currently have sixty-five students, whom I see weekly, twice a month, or once a month. How often I see them is dictated by their needs; younger ones I see more often.

What's the best part of your job?

The kids are great—I love them. They usually see you as someone on their side. In general, working with the patients and seeing their progress is a very gratifying feeling.

I also like the flexibility of the hours and the control I have over my own schedule. I get to move around to different locations, always learning different things and getting a broad perspective. It's really good if you have a family, and it's nice to have autonomy with your career.

What's the worst part of your job?

The lack of follow-through from other people, such as nurses, family members, caregivers, or teachers. It seems worse than it used to be because people can now Google things and think they know the answers. You have to justify and prove your expertise more now than ever. The paperwork can also be overwhelming sometimes.

What's the most surprising thing about your job?

How much I would love it and how passionate I would be—it's become a part of me. It influences and informs how I function in my life.

What kinds of qualities do you think one needs to be successful at this job?

Passion for the underdog! You must see potential in people beyond themselves and know how to motivate people. It's important to have compassion. Also, be organized yet flexible.

Did your education prepare you for the job?

Yes, especially the clinicals and the hands-on experience I got. Although the career requirements have changed since I graduated with a bachelor's degree. Now it's an entry-level master's degree. In 2021, it's becoming a doctorate program. The focus on research is very strong.

How do you combat burnout?

When you go to school for OT, they talk about your own self-care and figuring out your own work-life balance. Heed that advice. Try not to work at home if possible. Also, for me, exercise helps. I get summers off due to the school schedule.

My advice is to have something else other than your career and don't get too emotionally connected to your patients—this helps you make better decisions and avoid burnout.

What would you tell a young person who is thinking about becoming an OT?

Be sure to volunteer or job shadow with different OTs in different settings so you can actually see what the job really looks like. Get good grades—it's pretty competitive to get into school. They are looking for well-rounded people these days, so get experience and do things that interest you.

Making High School Count

Regardless of the career you choose, if you are interested in any of the allied health professions, there are some basic yet important things you can do while in high school to position yourself in the most advantageous way. Remember—it's not just about having the best application, it's also about figuring out what professions you actually would enjoy doing and which ones don't suit you.

- Load up on the sciences, especially biology. A head start in anatomy, biology, and/or physiology will be a big help in all allied health professions.
- Sign up for psychology. You treat the whole person, not just a body.
- Be comfortable using all kinds of computer software. It'll come in handy if you start your own practice.
- Learn first aid and CPR. You'll need these important skills regardless of your profession.
- Hone your communication skills in English, speech, and debate. You'll need them to speak with everyone from doctors to patients in pain.
- Volunteer in as many settings as you can. Read on to learn more about this important aspect of career planning.

> "It's a good idea to seek out volunteer work and get exposed to various aspects of physical therapy so you know what they are all like. Each area—hospital, private practice, sports medicine, pediatrics, women's health, neurologically impaired, etc.—has its pros and cons."—Jeff Busha, PT, MBA, MS, COMT, OCS

Educational Requirements

The nice thing is that no matter what degree of postsecondary education you can or want to pursue, there is a way for you to choose an allied health profession and be a part of the world of health and fitness. The following sections cover the big six professions of this book in more detail. Having said that, the general trend in the allied health careers is toward requiring higher-level degrees than in the past. The PT degree used to be a master's level degree and now it's a doctoral degree. The OT degree will soon also become a doctoral degree as well. If you graduate and meet the current requirements of your profession (and begin practicing and pass the state licensure requirements), you won't be expected to go back and earn that additional degree, as you'll be grandfathered in. At this stage of the planning process, you should just be aware of the current requirements and whether there are any plans to change them. (In many allied health professions, the educational requirements are in the process of becoming more rigorous.)

EDUCATIONAL REQUIREMENTS FOR A PHYSICAL THERAPIST

In order to be able to practice as a PT, you must earn a doctoral degree from an accredited academic program in physical therapy and pass your state's licensure exam. (Note that the doctoral degree was not always required, and if you speak with some PTs currently practicing, their schooling may be to the master's level only. All currently practicing PTs were grandfathered in.)

This is officially called the doctor of physical therapy (DPT) degree and it typically takes three years to complete, usually translating into 109–113 credit hours of graduate coursework. That's three additional years after graduating with an undergraduate degree in something like human biology or anatomy, kinesiology, exercise science, or athletic training. Other undergraduate degrees that prepare you for PT schooling might include developmental psychology, chemistry, and physiology. Some undergraduate schools even have a path called "pre-PT." Most, if not all, PT education programs require a bachelor's degree prior to admission into the DPT program.

Some universities offer what they call a "3+3 curricular format" in which you take three years of specific preprofessional (undergraduate/pre-PT) courses and then can advance into the three-year professional DPT program. These are often called hybrid programs. This assumes that you meet all academic requirements, which are usually quite rigorous. This program can potentially save you a year of schooling.

For universities in the United States, PT programs are accredited by the Commission on Accreditation in Physical Therapy Education (CAPTE). The point is to standardize and ensure the quality of the education that student PTs are receiving throughout the United States. As mentioned, you must attend a CAPTE-accredited program in order to practice as a PT in the United States (and Scotland). The list of accredited programs is very long; you can find the most updated version at aptaapps.apta.org/accreditedschoolsdirectory. You can search by state using a clickable map.

Licensing requirements vary by state, but all include passing the National Physical Therapy Examination administered by the Federation of State Boards of Physical Therapy (FSBPT). You can find the requirements of your resident state on the American Physical Therapy Association website at www.apta.org.

If you want to pursue the PT route, you need to be ready to work hard for the best grades you can get, be okay with spending hours in a lab, be ready to memorize parts of the body, and be able to master difficult scientific concepts. It's a competitive and academically rigorous field.

THE BENEFITS OF BECOMING A PHYSICAL THERAPIST ASSISTANT

If the degree requirements to become a PT seem daunting to you, consider the physical therapist assistant (PTA) track instead. PTAs do the job of a PT under the supervision and direction of licensed PTs. PTAs entering the profession only need an associate's degree from an accredited program. In addition, all states require PTAs to be licensed or certified. If desired, you can use your PTA experience and on-the-job training to later enter PT school, all the while earning a living.

EDUCATIONAL REQUIREMENTS FOR AN OCCUPATIONAL THERAPIST

In order to be able to practice as an OT, you must earn a master's degree from an accredited academic program in occupational therapy, pass the national board exam, and gain a license to practice in your resident state. The master's degree is typically two additional years after graduating with an undergraduate degree in something like sociology, psychology, kinesiology, exercise science, or anthropology. Most, if not all, OT education programs require a bachelor's degree prior to admission into the program.

Potential OTs spend their years earning their master's degree learning about anatomy, patient care, social/medical conditions, and assistive technologies in their field. During this time, fieldwork is critical. Fieldwork can take place in settings like schools, nursing homes, rehab centers, or even private practices. It takes about twenty-four weeks on average to complete the fieldwork.[1]

OT fieldwork is broken into Level I and Level II experiences. Level I fieldwork is intended for new students to help them become comfortable with patients. Level II affords the student more autonomy with patients and, according to the American Occupational Therapy Association (AOTA), "must be integral to the program's curriculum design and must include an in-depth experience in delivering occupational therapy services to clients, focusing on the application of purposeful and meaningful occupations."[2] A general guideline is to observe under at least three therapists in three different settings. For more information, check out the AOTA website at www.aota.org.

The final step after receiving your degrees is to get your state OT license, which requires completion of a certain number of hours of accredited fieldwork (usually twenty-four weeks of full-time Level II fieldwork) and passing the National Board for Certification in Occupational Therapy exam. Once you meet these requirements, you are granted the OTR credential.

Just as with the PT field, becoming an OT is a very competitive and selective process. You need to be ready to work hard for the best grades you can get, volunteer/shadow as much as you can manage, and be able to master difficult scientific concepts. As mentioned earlier, the educational requirements are likely to get steeper soon. Note that by 2025, the AOTA reports that a doctoral degree will be considered the entry-level educational requirement for OTs.

The OT profession also has an assistant role. The occupational therapy assistant (OTA) performs support activities for the OT in charge. This can be a good way to gain hands-on experience in the field and then later enter OT school if you want, earning a living at the same time.

EDUCATIONAL REQUIREMENTS FOR A RECREATIONAL THERAPIST

Recreational therapists (RTs) can enter the profession with several different levels of education. The most basic degree is the associate's degree in recreational therapy. This two-year degree qualifies you for an entry-level job in the recreation therapy field, whereby you provide support activities under the supervision of a certified therapeutic recreation specialist (CTRS). If you pursue an associate's degree, you'll take classes related to patient interaction and learn about the historical, practical, and theoretical components of recreational therapy.[3] These programs also typically require fieldwork, where you gain that all-important hands-on experience. Along with the main recreational therapy classes, you will take therapy-focused courses in music, drama, social dance, and art. Note that you cannot become a certified recreational therapist (CRT) with this level of education; for that, you need at least a bachelor's. However, the associate's degree is a very good way to gain practical experience that you can apply to entry-level positions or use to further your education while earning a living.

A bachelor's degree in recreational therapy prepares you to become a CRT. With this degree, you also have to complete internships and fieldwork under the supervision of a CTRS. In fact, you'll need approximately 480 hours of supervised recreational therapy internship work, usually over a prescribed number of weeks. The exact number of hours depends on the state in which you will be certified.

The bachelor's degree curriculum includes classes related to therapeutic recreation, physical and behavioral sciences, and recreation and leisure administration. General science education requirements, such as anatomy and physiology, are also part of the coursework.[4]

A master's degree in recreational therapy typically requires one to two years of additional study after the bachelor's degree. The coursework focuses on management and administration and covers the assessment and evaluation of patient health, human development, and program-planning study.[5] You will also be involved in fieldwork and will be expected to conduct advanced research in the field.

Note that many employers require that their RTs be certified. To be certified, you must earn at least a bachelor's degree, complete an internship in the field, and then pass an exam.

EDUCATIONAL REQUIREMENTS FOR AN EXERCISE PHYSIOLOGIST

Unlike with the previous professional tracks, there is no national, standardized education track that you have to follow to become an exercise physiologist (EP). This is due in part to the fact that this is a more recent profession in the allied health arena. However, getting a bachelor's degree in exercise science, kinesiology, anatomy, physiology, nutrition, or a related area is considered an entry-level requirement to be an EP. Typical coursework includes classes such as gerontology, pharmacology, and abnormal psychology.

Universities usually offer one or a combination of the following four study tracks to major in exercise physiology: clinical (applied), clinical (research), human performance, and pre-health professional.[6] Mirroring the general trend toward higher educational degrees, healthcare facilities are increasingly requiring that their EPs hold master's degrees. Some programs offer a fifth-year master's degree option.

Along with making you more marketable, master's programs allow you to gain knowledge about the specific field in which you want to work. During your master's program, you have the opportunity to hold an internship and gain more hands-on experience. Of course, the American Society of Exercise Physiologists (ASEP) recommends you look for an accredited degree program, regardless of your degree type.

In addition to a bachelor's or master's degree, there are several certifications available that make you more marketable and well-rounded as an EP. These include credentials through the ASEP, the American College of Sports Medicine (ACSM), the National Academy of Sports Medicine (NASM), or the Cooper Institute. Although these certifications are not mandatory, most employers require at least one, depending on the particulars of your work environment.

EDUCATIONAL REQUIREMENTS FOR A MASSAGE THERAPIST

To become a massage therapist, you need to earn a certificate in massage therapy, which typically involves 500–1,000 hours of academic and clinical work. The magic number of hours required varies by state. This translates to about one to two years of schooling. You don't need to pursue a bachelor's degree or attend college to become certified. Finding a school or program that offers massage therapy degrees near you is usually not a problem, but be sure you pick a reputable one that is recognized by your state's licensing board. Most states require massage therapists to be licensed, which involves sitting for an exam.

To make sure you are maximally marketable, get certified in as many massage modalities as possible. These are basically types of massage that you are licensed to perform. Examples include Swedish, deep-tissue, cupping, infant, prenatal, taping, and ortho-bionomy. The more well-rounded you are in this regard, the more marketable you'll be to companies looking to hire you and the easier it will be to build your client base.

During your schooling, but after you've taken a set minimum number of classes, you will learn your craft by giving on-the-job massages to real clients. You will often receive a portion of the fee charged for the massage (the school gets the lion's share). So you are in school, practicing your craft, and can earn a little money too.

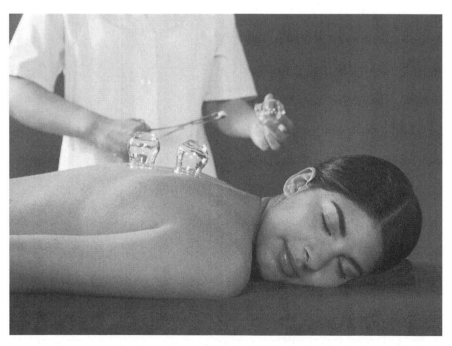

Young woman getting cupping treatment

MAKING CONNECTIONS WHILE MAKING
PEOPLE FEEL BETTER

Quintin Rupard

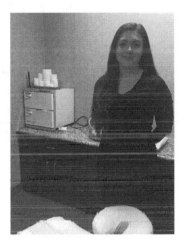

Kaitlyn Steiner

Quintin Rupard is a licensed massage therapist (LMT) and Kaitlyn Steiner is a certified massage therapist (CMT). They both work at a large national health and fitness center. Quintin and Kaitlyn were interviewed together.

What's a typical day for you on the job?

Quintin: I like to come in and get the room ready for my first client, such as turning on the table warmer and hot stones and aroma therapy diffuser, and then I meet the client and lead them to the room. I always ask clients about any injuries, medications, etc., to base the massage off of their needs and wants. Massages can be thirty, sixty, or ninety minutes at the club where I work, and I enjoy giving the sixty-minute ones the most because you get the most out of it without getting too repetitive. I often do four to six massages per day typically. My feet and knees can hurt after a long day of standing, as well as my neck from looking down so long. If you do the massage properly, you won't injure yourself.

Kaitlyn: I have worked more with geriatric bodies, which I enjoy. I also worked at a dental office that gave hand and foot massages during their teeth cleanings. I am new at the club, so my goal is to start with four massages a day. I am working about seventeen hours weekly at first, and as you go along, you build your client base and your physical tolerance for giving massages.

How do you acquire clients?

Quintin: I get referrals from trainers at the club, who refer their clients who have an issue. Networking with trainers is smart. I also get random assignments from people who call in and then they hopefully stick with me from that point on.

Kaitlyn: Word of mouth is the best way, because people trust their friends' opinions. When my clients like my massages and tell their friends, that's a great way to build a base. You can do advertising, but it costs money and is probably less effective. With friend referrals, it's more likely to be repeat clients as well, which is always better. You can see progress if you have a returning client.

What is cupping? It's a specialized form of massage whereby the therapists applies special cups to the skin to create suction in areas troubled by inflammation, blood flow, and pain. It is an ancient form of alternative Chinese medicine that dates back thousands of years.

What kinds of massage are you certified for?

Quintin: Swedish, deep-tissue, prenatal, infant, cupping, and taping.

Kaitlyn: Swedish, ortho-bionomy, and cupping.

What is ortho-bionomy massage? This is a gentle, noninvasive method of massage that's been shown to be effective at relieving stress and addressing injuries related to improper posture issues. It's a good example of a massage modality that has recently become very popular.

What's the best part of your job?

Quintin: All of it! Psychological effects of having people open up to you; help[ing] people mentally and physically; and seeing the effects of how a massage can relieve pain and they can move parts of their body so much better, without pain.

People come in with injuries and you can help them get better to the point where they don't need surgery, as long as they keep up with the massages.

Kaitlyn: Making people more self-aware of how their body functions. Help[ing] them make connections with how they sleep, use of muscles, how they sit and generally treat their body, and how they feel because of that.

What's the worst or most challenging part of your job?

Quintin: No-shows! It doesn't happen too often, but it's weekly. Also, as a man in the field, you have to deal with the fact that not as many people want a massage from a man. Men prefer women and women often also prefer women. This is where word of mouth is even more important, especially when a trainer recommends you.

Kaitlyn: No-shows, yes. Starting out is challenging—you have to work hard to build your client base. Also, sometimes people get the wrong idea about what it means to get a massage, and they think you are open to prostitution.

What's the most surprising thing about your job?

Quintin: How quickly the friendships often develop with clients. You spend an hour with them at a time and you get to know them well.

Did your education prepare you for the job?

Kaitlyn: Carmel Massage School, 500 credit hours (one year) clinical (on-site) and class.

Quintin: Indiana Massage School, 750 credit hours.

Is the job what you expected?

Quintin: Better than I expected due to relationships, build[ing] clientele quicker than I thought.

Kaitlyn: Hands-on clinical helps you know what it will be like.

How do you combat burnout?

Quintin: Get massages regularly. Have boundaries with people to avoid mental burnout—you are not their emotional trash can.

Kaitlyn: Use proper body mechanics at all times to not injure yourself; table height is important, for example.

What would you tell a young person who is thinking about pursuing this career?

Quintin: A lot more work than you think; the educational aspect is a lot too, although about a year in school. You have freedom over your schedule; you can work less hours if you want. Learn as many modalities as you can as quickly as you can, especially ones that will make you more marketable.

Kaitlyn: More like a trade, which is nice; don't have to go to college—no college debt. School is affordable compared to the living you make.

EDUCATIONAL REQUIREMENTS FOR AN ATHLETIC TRAINER

To become an athletic trainer, you need a degree in athletic training from an accredited program and then you must pass the national board of certification (BOC) exam. At this point in time, the degree can be either a bachelor's or master's degree, depending on your focus. However, the Athletic Training Strategic Alliance (ATSA) recently announced that the degree, like so many others in the allied health field, will be moving to a master's level in the coming years.[7] In fact, according to the National Athletic Trainers Association, more than 70 percent of athletic trainers hold at least a master's degree at this point in time.[8] The exact implementation date for the change has not yet been determined, so be sure to do some searching online to get the latest information before you make a decision. Some websites to check include the National Athletic Trainers Association) website at www.nata.org and the Commission on Accreditation of Athletic Training Education (CAATE) website at caate.net.

The athletic trainer degree is a very specific degree. Note that similar degrees in areas like physical therapy, exercise science, or others will not qualify you to sit for the BOC examination and become a licensed athletic trainer.

Accredited programs in the United States include education in areas such as injury/illness prevention, first aid and emergency treatment, nutrition, physiology, injury/illness assessment, human anatomy, and therapeutic techniques. Along with classes and book instruction, you'll have many hours of hands-on clinical education experiences.

> "I can't stress enough that sincerity, passion, and kindness are all very important. You need to be gentle and kind to people who don't exercise and have an issue with their bodies and a block about feeling good. You have to get the mind before you get the body."—Sharon Phillips, athletic trainer

In addition to the BOC exam, most states also have their own credentials that you must obtain in order to practice there. The CAATE is the body that certifies schools. Its website has lots of good information about becoming an athletic trainer, including the three different levels of accreditation for schools, information about the BOC exam, and a search capability that allows you to search for programs in your area that meet the credentials.

Experience-Related Requirements

This section covers the required fieldwork of each profession, which is the fieldwork and/or internship work you'll do during the course of your education. It also discusses other ways you can get experience in the field before and during the time you're pursuing a degree. This can and should start in middle school or high school, especially during the summers. Experience is important for many reasons:

- Shadowing others in the profession can help reveal what the job is really like and whether it's something that you think you want to do, day in and day out. This is a relatively risk-free way to explore different career paths. Ask any seasoned adult and he or she will tell you that figuring out what you *don't* want to do is sometimes more important than figuring out what you do want to do.

- Internships and volunteer work are a relatively quick way to gain work experience and develop job skills.
- Volunteering can help you learn the intricacies of the profession, such as what types of environments are best, what kind of care fits you better, and which areas are in more demand.
- Gaining experience during your high school years sets you apart from the many others who are applying to college. These are competitive fields, and it shows admissions boards that you're serious and understand what's expected of you when you have some volunteering or shadowing experience under your belt.
- Volunteering in the field means that you'll be meeting many others doing the job that you might someday want to do (think: career networking). You have the potential to develop mentor relationships, cultivate future job prospects, and get to know people who can recommend you for later positions. Studies show that about 85 percent of jobs are found through personal contacts.[9]

Experience can come in the form of volunteering at the local clinic or in your community, taking on an internship in the summer, finding a summer job that complements your interests, or even attending camps that foster your career aspirations. (See the TeenLife site at www.teenlife.com to start.) Consider these tidbits of advice to maximize your volunteer experience.[10] They will help you stand out in competitive fields:

- Get diverse experiences. For example, for OT and PT experience, try to get experience in at least two or three different settings, such as rehab centers, schools, hospitals, and outpatient settings.
- Try to gain forty hours of volunteer experience in each setting. This is typically considered enough to show that you understand what a full work week looks like in that setting. This can be as few as four to five hours per week over ten weeks or so.
- If your profession has such a job, find an aide/tech position. Working as a paid aide is by far the best experience you can get. This will prepare you nicely for your clinical experiences in college as well.
- Don't be afraid to ask questions. Just be considerate of the professionals' time and wait until they are not busy to pursue your questions. Asking good questions shows that you have a real curiosity for the profession.

- Maintain and cultivate professional relationships. Write thank-you notes, send updates about your application progress and tell them where you decide to go to school, and check in occasionally. If you want to find a good mentor, you need to be a gracious and willing mentee.

GETTING EXPERIENCE IN PHYSICAL THERAPY

If you're currently in high school and you're seriously thinking about pursuing the DPT degree, it would be smart to volunteer at a hospital or another health-care facility. The benefit of volunteering is that it's much easier to get your foot in the door, but the drawback is that you typically will not be paid. However, with time and hard work, your volunteer position may turn into something else. Look at these kinds of experiences as ways to learn about the profession, show people how capable you are, and make connections with others that could last your career. It may even help you to get into the college of your choice, and it will definitely help you write your personal statement as to why you want to be a PT.

To find such positions, start with your high school guidance counselor or website, visit the websites listed in this book, reach out to family friends, and search the web for clinics, hospitals, schools, and private practices in your area. Don't be afraid to pick up the phone and call them. Be prepared to start by cleaning facilities, assisting staff with clerical work, and other such tasks. Being on-site, no matter what you're doing, will teach you more than you know. With a great attitude and work ethic, you will likely be given more responsibility over time.

Once you are in school, you will get many hours of hands-on experience as well. In addition to the eight semesters of study, the DPT degree incorporates thirty-two weeks of a full-time clinical internship. This equates to about 22 credit hours out of approximately 109 of a clinical internship through your university. At this point, you will have a good idea as to which setting you want to work in, so you should use those clinical internships wisely to experiment and gain knowledge about your profession.

GETTING EXPERIENCE IN OCCUPATIONAL THERAPY

If you're currently in high school and you're seriously thinking about becoming an OT, start by volunteering. OTs are found at hospitals and healthcare facilities as well as schools and nursing homes. The benefit of volunteering is that it's much easier to get your foot in the door, but the drawback is that you typically will not be paid. Starting with school districts may be more promising, and people in the educational field generally understand the need to teach others and may value that effort more than others.

Remember that with time and hard work, your volunteer position may turn into something else. Look at these kinds of experiences as ways to learn about the profession, show people how capable you are, and make connections with others that could last your career. As with the PT position, volunteer experience may help you to get into the college of your choice. Contact your high school counselor, visit the websites listed in this book, and search the web for clinics, hospitals, schools, and private practices in your area. Try calling the human resources department of local businesses for information as well. If you live in or near a college town, don't hesitate to use the university's connections and services.

> "I started [my OT career] by working with adults. I actually got a job while I was still in college [with a nursing home]. They gave me money to finish school if I would come work for them."—Laura Isaacs, OTR

Once you are in school, you will be required to get many hours of hands-on experience as well. OT fieldwork, broken into Level I and Level II experiences, can take place in settings like schools, nursing homes, rehab centers, or even private practices. It takes about twenty-four weeks on average to complete the fieldwork.[11] A general guideline is to observe under at least three therapists in three different settings. These internships are set up and arranged through your university, and this is your last stop before becoming a full-fledged OT!

GETTING EXPERIENCE IN THE RECREATIONAL THERAPY

As with many of the professions discussed in this book, full internships and fieldwork opportunities are usually open only to college and graduate students currently studying the field. If you're in high school and looking to find some experience in recreational therapy, you might have to get creative. Community service and volunteering are good places to start. Consider camps, nursing homes, and even the Meals on Wheels program. Knowing that you will take therapy-focused courses in music, drama, social dance, and art, how can you turn a job as a camp counselor into something that trains and prepares you for a life as an RT?

As with the other positions, you can approach your high school counselor, visit the websites listed in this book, and search the web for clinics, schools, camps, and nursing homes in your area. Reach out to local RTs and ask to interview them as a start to building a relationship and filling in your knowledge gaps.

Regardless of the level of degree you decide to pursue here, during your studies you will have the opportunity to complete internships and fieldwork under the supervision of a CRT. With these internships, which are set up and managed by your university or college, you'll gain hands-on experience and earn class credits.

GETTING EXPERIENCE IN EXERCISE PHYSIOLOGY

If you're currently in high school and you're seriously thinking about becoming an EP, it's a good idea to get some experience by volunteering. The benefit of volunteering is that it's much easier to find a job, but the drawback is that you typically will not be paid. However, if you can find four to five hours per week to volunteer in your desired field, you will reap benefits during college admissions that could end up saving you money, and certainly will save you some anguish.

To find a volunteer or internship position, start where you live and with what you know. If you are or have been part of a school or athletic team, start by approaching the coaching team about your aspirations. It always helps when people know you and respect your work ethic. Look at these kinds of experiences as ways to learn about the profession, show people how capable you are, and make connections with others that could last your career. As with the other positions, you can approach your high school counselor, visit the websites listed in this book, and search the web for clinics, schools, local research facilities, and even gyms in your area. Don't be afraid to pick up the phone. If you live in or near a college town, don't hesitate to use the university's connections and services. Opportunities often exist for students to engage in undergraduate research activities with faculty members, and many universities offer summer internships in the health and fitness arena.

The exercise science field, more so than some others, is experientially based. Most schools require that exercise science majors participate in at least one internship experience. Internship opportunities exist in various areas that fall under exercise science, such as cardiac rehabilitation, corporate fitness, wellness and fitness centers, strength and conditioning programs, and sport-specific conditioning programs, as well as in other areas you're interested in. With exercise physiology, you have the opportunity to get creative and build your own internship that matches your interests and areas of exercise physiology. Since the degree can and will differ across the student population, your body of volunteer work is even more important to set you apart from the rest.

GETTING EXPERIENCE IN MASSAGE THERAPY

Unlike the other allied health professions discussed in this book, massage therapy does not require a full postsecondary degree; you simply need to earn a certificate in massage therapy, which typically involves 500–1,000 hours of academic and clinical work, depending on the state in which you want to practice. Most schools require a high school diploma.

The clinical work involves a considerable number of hours spent on-site at the school in the activity of giving massages (this is intentionally vague because requirements depend on the state). Typically, you will first observe a licensed massage therapist for a prescribed number of hours, then you can begin to give massages to family and friends to get practice, then you give massages to actual clients of the school (sometimes with supervision), and then you move on to being able to give massages on your own. During the middle stages, you typically retain a portion of the fee charged (the school gets the rest). At the final stage, many schools treat students as independent contractors; students keep all the money they earn and pay a fee to the school to rent the room. This prepares therapists to move next into the real world of massage therapy, and it's all certified through your school.

Because most states require massage therapists to be licensed, you can't really volunteer at places of work unless you are working in a support capacity (cleaning rooms and washing towels, for example). It's arguably a better use of your time to work your clinicals in school and actually be able to give massages under supervision. If you're in high school and thinking about massage therapy, research the schools in your area and determine which ones have the best reputations. Be sure they are state-accredited as well. Scour their websites, then visit and bring questions. Make sure that on-site, literally hands-on clinical work is a big part of the instruction.

Because your goal should be to get certified in as many massage modalities as are lucrative and interesting to you, continuing education and clinical experience is very important. Keep up with the latest advances and get certified when you can. In the field of massage therapy, this ongoing experience and certification is more important than gaining experience while you are in school. You'll do that anyway if you attend a licensed, reputable school.

GETTING EXPERIENCE IN ATHLETIC TRAINING

If you are currently in high school and are considering the athletic training profession, you can find volunteering opportunities in your community similar to the ones described in the section about exercise physiology. It's always smart to start where you live and with what you know. For example, if you are or have been part of a school or athletic team, start by approaching the coaching team about your aspirations and ask them about what kinds of support roles you could take on to learn and to help the team.

Look at these kinds of experiences as ways to learn about the profession, show people how capable you are, and make connections with others that could last your career. Contact your high school counselor, visit the websites listed in this book, and search the web for clinics, schools, local research facilities, and fitness facilities in your area. Finally, don't be afraid to pick up the phone. Put yourself out there and be professional and courteous.

The athletic trainer degree is a very specific degree. Note that similar degrees in areas like physical therapy, exercise science, or others will not qualify you to sit for the exam and become a licensed athletic trainer. However, lots of different kinds of experience can help you understand this profession better and will count as training in the field. For example, being a camp counselor during your summers can even be a good "in" to athletic training.

Shadow your school's athletic trainer for a day, or visit the local physical therapy/ sports medicine clinic and make yourself available for volunteer work.

Once you are pursuing your degree, as with the other allied health professions, you will have many opportunities to take on internships and do fieldwork. Students at accredited schools who are studying athletic training have many opportunities to gain hands-on athletic training experience while pursuing their degree, all arranged through their university.

Networking

Because it's so important, another last word about networking: It's important to develop mentor relationships even at this stage. Remember that about 85 percent of jobs are found through personal contacts. If you know someone in the field, don't hesitate to reach out. Be patient and polite, but ask for help, perspective, and guidance. If you don't know anyone, ask your school guidance counselor to help you make connections. Or pick up the phone yourself. Reaching out with a genuine interest in knowledge and a real curiosity about the field will go a long way. You don't need a job or an internship just yet—just a connection that could blossom into a mentoring relationship. Follow these important but simple rules for the best results when networking:

- Do your homework about a potential contact, connection, university, or employer before you make contact. Be sure to have a general understanding of what they do and why. But don't be a know-it-all. Be open and ready to ask good questions.
- Be considerate of professionals' time and resources. Think about what they can get from you in return for mentoring or helping you.
- Speak and write using proper English. Proofread all your letters, e-mails, and even texts. Think about how you will be perceived at all times.
- Always stay positive.

Summary

In this chapter, you learned even more about six different careers in the health and fitness umbrella—physical therapy, occupational therapy, recreational therapy, exercise physiology, massage therapy, and athletic training. You've learned all about the educational requirements of these six different careers, from postsecondary certificates to doctoral degrees. You also learned about getting experience in these professions before you enter school as well as during the educational process. At this time, you should have a good idea of the educational requirements of each career. You hopefully even contemplated some questions about what kind of educational career path fits your strengths, time requirements, and wallet. Are you starting to picture your career plan? If not, that's okay, as there's still time.

Remember that no matter which of these professions you pursue, you must maintain current certifications and meet continuing education requirements. Advances in understanding in the fields of medicine, kinesiology, nutrition, and more are continuous, and it's important that you keep apprised of what's happening in your field.

Chapter 3 goes into a lot more detail about pursing the best educational path. The chapter covers the best schools for each profession, as well as how to find the best value for your education, and includes a discussion about financial aid and scholarships. At the end of chapter 3, you should have a much clearer view of the educational landscape and how and where you fit in.

3

Pursuing the Education Path

*W*hen it comes time to start looking at colleges, universities, or postsecondary schools, many high schoolers tend to freeze up at the enormity of the job ahead of them. This chapter will help break down this process for you so it won't seem so daunting.

It's true that finding the right college or learning institution is an important one, and it's a big step toward achieving your career goals and dreams. The last chapter covered the various educational requirements of these six professions, which means you should now be ready to find the right institution of learning. This isn't always just a process of finding the very best school that you can afford and can be accepted into, although that might end up being your path. It should also be about finding the right fit so that you can have the best possible experience during your post–high school years.

But here's the truth of it all: postsecondary schooling isn't just about getting a degree. It's about learning how to be an adult, managing your life and your responsibilities, being exposed to new experiences, growing as a person, and otherwise moving toward becoming an adult who contributes to society. College offers you an opportunity to actually become an interesting person with perspective on the world and empathy and consideration for people other than yourself, if you let it.

An important component of how successful you will be in college is finding the right fit, the right school that brings out the best in you and challenges you at different levels. I know—no pressure, right? Just as with finding the right profession, your ultimate goal should be to match your personal interests, goals, and personality with the college's goals and perspective. For example, small liberal arts colleges have a much different feel and philosophy than Big 10 state schools. And rest assured that all this advice applies even if you're planning on attending community college or massage therapy school.

Don't worry, though: in addition to these soft skills, this chapter does dive into the nitty-gritty of how to find the best school, no matter what you want to do. In the allied health field specifically, attending an accredited program is critical to future success, and that is covered in detail in this chapter.

Finding a College That Fits Your Personality

Before looking at the details of good schools for each profession, it will behoove you to take some time to consider what type of school will be best for you. Answering questions like the ones that follow can help you narrow your search and focus on a smaller set of choices. Write your answers to these questions down somewhere where you can refer to them often, such as in your notes app on your phone.

- *Size:* Does the size of the school matter to you? Colleges and universities range in size from five hundred or fewer students to twenty-five thousand students.
- *Community location:* Would you prefer to be in a rural area, a small town, a suburban area, or a large city? How important is the location of the school in the larger world?
- *Distance from home:* How far away from home—in terms of hours or miles away—do you want/are you willing to go?
- *Housing options:* What kind of housing would you prefer? Dorms, off-campus apartments, and private homes are all common options.
- *Student body:* How would you like the student body to look? Think about coed versus all-male and all-female settings, as well as ethnic diversity, how many students are part-time versus full-time, and the percentage of commuter students.
- *Academic environment:* Which majors are offered, and at which degree levels? Research the student-faculty ratio. Are the classes taught often by actual professors or more often by the teaching assistants? How many internships does the school typically provide to students? Are independent study or study abroad programs available in your area of interest?

- *Financial aid availability/cost:* Does the school provide ample opportunities for scholarships, grants, work-study programs, and the like? Does cost play a role in your options? (For most people, it does.)
- *Support services:* How strong are the school's academic and career placement counseling services?
- *Social activities and athletics:* Does the school offer clubs that you are interested in? Which sports are offered? Are scholarships available?
- *Specialty programs:* Does the school offer honors programs or programs for veterans or students with disabilities or special needs?

Not all of these questions are going to be important to you, and that's fine. Be sure to make note of aspects that don't matter as much to you. You might change your mind as you visit colleges, but it's important to make note of where you are to begin with.

Finding a college or school setting that fits your needs, wants, and personality is an important indicator of success.

U.S. News & World Report puts it best when it reports that the college that fits you best is one that:

- Offers a degree that matches your interests and needs
- Provides a style of instruction that matches the way you like to learn
- Provides a level of academic rigor to match your aptitude and preparation
- Offers a community that feels like home to you
- Values you for what you do well[1]

According to the National Center for Educational Statistics (NCES), which is part of the US Department of Education, six years after entering college for an undergraduate degree, only 59 percent of students have graduated.[2] Barely half of those students will graduate from college in their lifetime.[3]

Hopefully, this section has impressed upon you the importance of finding the right college fit. Take some time to paint a mental picture of the kind of university or school setting that will best complement your needs. Then read on for specifics about each degree.

HOW IMPORTANT IS ACCREDITATION?

Keep in mind that many companies will hire only people who hold a degree from a program that has specific accreditation. This is especially true in the allied health professions, which are more heavily regulated. When you research a school, make sure you can verify that the program of study is accredited through the proper accreditation body (and that it's still active and valid). As discussed in previous chapters, some credentials are granted through state agencies and some through national boards, so you need to do a little research on your area of interest.

For more information on accreditation programs in general, visit these sites:

- The Accrediting Bureau of Health Education Schools at www.abhes.org. This accrediting agency is recognized by the US Department of Education and by the Council for Higher Education Accreditation.
- The Association of Schools of Allied Health Professions at www.asahp.org. This not-for-profit professional association's members include administrators, educators, and others who are concerned with issues that affect allied health education.
- The Commission on Accreditation of Allied Health Education Programs at www.caahep.org. This organization claims to be the largest programmatic accreditor in the health sciences field.[4]

Your Degree Plan for Studies in Allied Health

If you're in high school and you are serious about pursuing a degree in physical therapy (a doctoral degree), occupational therapy (a master's degree), recreational therapy (an associate's, bachelor's, or master's degree), exercise physiology (usually a master's degree), or athletic training (a bachelor's or master's degree), start by finding five to ten schools in a realistic location (for you) that offer the degree you want to pursue. Not every school near you or that you have an initial interest in will grant the degree you want, of course, so narrow your choices accordingly. With that said, consider attending a university in your resident state, if possible; you will save lots of money if you attend a state school. Private institutions don't typically discount resident student tuition costs.

Be sure you research the basic grade point average (GPA) and SAT or ACT requirements of each school as well. This discussion assumes that you meet the basic academic requirements, which are very rigorous for the doctor of physical therapy (DPT) and occupational therapist (OT) programs, and are less so— but still very competitive—for the others.

Most advisors recommend that students take both the ACT and the SAT during the spring of their junior year at the latest. (The ACT is generally considered more heavily weighted in science, so it may be more important when you're applying to allied health programs.) You can retake these tests and use your highest score, so be sure to leave time for a retake early in your senior year if needed. You want your best score to be available to all the schools you're applying to by January of your senior year, which will also enable your score to be considered with any scholarship applications. Keep in mind these are general timelines—be sure to check the exact deadlines and calendars of the schools to which you're applying!

Once you have found five to ten schools in a realistic location that offer the degree you are looking for, spend some time on their websites studying the requirements for admission. Most universities list the average stats for the last class accepted to each program. Important factors in your decision about what schools to apply to should include whether or not you meet the requirements, your chances of getting in (but shoot high!), tuition costs and availability of scholarships and grants, location, and the school's reputation and licensure/ graduation rates.

The importance of these characteristics will depend on your grades and test scores, your financial resources, and other personal factors. You want to find a university that has a good reputation for the science and health fields, but it's also important to match your academic rigor and practical needs with the best school you can.

Remember too that some universities offer hybrid programs that can save you a year or so of schooling. For example, schools that offer the DPT degree may have a "3+3 curricular format" in which you take three years of specific preprofessional (undergraduate/pre-physical therapist [PT]) courses and then can move into the three-year professional DPT program. These types of programs save you time and money.

Note that the massage therapy schooling and certification process is covered separately later in this chapter, since it involves a different path than a full university degree.

THE MOST PERSONAL OF PERSONAL STATEMENTS

The personal statement you include with your application to college is extremely important, especially if your GPA and SAT/ACT scores are on the border of what is typically accepted. Write something that is thoughtful and conveys your understanding of the profession you are interested in, as well as your desire to practice in this field. Why are you uniquely qualified? Why are you a good fit for the university? These essays should be highly personal (the "personal" in personal statement). Will the admissions professionals who read it—along with hundreds of others—come away with a snapshot of who you really are and what you are passionate about?

Look online for some examples of good personal statements, which will give you a feel for what works. Be sure to check your specific school for length guidelines, format requirements, and any other guidelines they expect you to follow.

And of course, be sure to proofread it several times and ask a professional (such as your school writing center or your local library services) to proofread it as well.

What's It Going to Cost You?

So, the bottom line: what will your education end up costing you? Of course, this depends on many factors, including the type and length of degree you pursue, where you attend (in-state or not, private or public institution), how much in scholarships or financial aid you're able to obtain, your family or personal income, and many other factors. The College Entrance Examination Board tracks and summarizes financial data from colleges and universities all over the United States. (You can find more information at www.collegeboard .org.) A sample of the most recent data is shown in the tables 3.1 and 3.2.

Table 3.1. Average Yearly Tuition, Fees, Room, and Board for Full-Time Undergraduates

Year	Public 2-Year	Public 4-Year, In-State	Public 4-Year, Out of State	Private Nonprofit
2016–2017	$11,640	$20,150	$35,300	$45,370
2017–2018	$11,970	$20,770	$36,420	$46,950

Source: College Entrance Examination Board website, https://trends.collegeboard.org/content/ average-published-tuition-and-fees-room-and-board-and-total-charges-institution-type (accessed March 10, 2018).

Table 3.2. Average Yearly Tuition, Fees, Room, and Board for Graduate Studies

Year	Doctorate, Public University	Doctorate, Private University	Master's Degree, Public University	Master's Degree, Private University
2016–2017	$10,510	$41,340	$8,360	$28,930
2017–2018	$10,830	$42,920	$8,670	$29,960

Source: College Entrance Examination Board website, https://trends.collegeboard.org/content/ average-published-tuition-and-fees-room-and-board-and-total-charges-institution-type (accessed March 10, 2018).

Keep in mind these are averages. If you read more specific data about a particular university or find averages in your particular area of interest, you should assume those numbers are closer to reality than these, as they are more specific. This data helps to show you the ballpark figures.

Generally speaking, there is about a 3 percent annual increase in tuition and associated costs to attend college. In other words, if you are expecting to attend college two years after this data was collected, you need to add approximately 6 percent to these numbers. Keep in mind that this assumes no financial aid or scholarships of any kind.

This chapter discusses finding the most affordable path to get the degree you want. Later in this chapter, you'll also learn how to prime the pumps and get as much money for college as you can.

WHAT IS A GAP YEAR?

Taking a year off between high school and college, often called a gap year, is normal, perfectly acceptable, and almost required in many countries around the world. It is becoming increasingly acceptable in the United States as well. Even Malia Obama, President Obama's daughter, did it. Because the cost of college has gone up dramatically, it literally pays for you to know going in what you want to study, and a gap year—well spent—can do lots to help you answer that question.

Some great ways to spend your gap year include joining organizations such as the Peace Corps or AmeriCorps, enrolling in a mountaineering program or other gap year–styled program, backpacking across Europe or other countries on the cheap (be safe and bring a friend), finding a volunteer organization that furthers a cause you believe in or that complements your career aspirations, joining a Road Scholar program (see www.roadscholar.org), teaching English in another country (more information available at www.gooverseas.com/blog/best-countries-for-seniors-to-teach-english -abroad), or working and earn money for college!

Many students find that they get much more out of college when they have a year to mature and to experience the real world. The American Gap Year Association reports from alumni surveys that students who take gap years show improved civic engagement, improved college graduation rates, and improved GPAs in college.[5] See the association's website at gapyearassociation.org for lots of advice and resources if you're considering this potentially life-altering experience.

Physical Therapy: Degree Required and Statistical Data

In order to practice in the United States as a PT, you currently need a doctor of physical therapy degree. This typically takes three additional years to complete, usually translating into 109–113 credit hours of graduate coursework, after graduating with an undergraduate degree in physical therapy or something like human biology or anatomy, kinesiology, exercise science, or athletic training. All states also require PTs to be licensed; licensing requirements vary by state.

The US Bureau of Labor Statistics (BLS)[6] reports that the average pay for a PT in 2016 (the most recent data at the time of this writing) was $85,400. The job growth/outlook for the decade 2016–2026 is 28 percent, which is much faster than average. This is universally considered a very good, viable, growing field.

GREAT SCHOOLS FOR PHYSICAL THERAPY

There are many different ways to judge something as "great," "the best," and so forth. What might be a great school for you might be too difficult, too expensive, or not rigorous enough for someone else. Keep in mind the advice of the previous sections when deciding what you really need in a school.

As one example of the way things can be ranked, here are some of the top schools for physical therapy, ranked and compiled in 2016 by *U.S. News & World Report*:

- University of Delaware (www.udel.edu)
- University of Pittsburgh (www.pitt.edu)
- University of Southern California (www.usc.edu)
- Washington University in St. Louis (wustl.edu)
- Emory University (www.emory.edu)
- Northwestern University (www.northwestern.edu)
- University of Iowa (www.uiowa.edu)
- MGH Institute of Health Professions (www.mghihp.edu)
- US Army–Baylor University (www.baylor.edu)
- Duke University in (www.duke.edu)
- The Ohio State University (www.osu.edu)
- University of Florida (www.ufl.edu)
- University of Miami (www.miami.edu)[7]

These rankings are based on peer assessments from other schools' professors, professionals, and deans. Only fully accredited programs in good standing during the survey period were ranked.

These schools represent a nice variety of geographical locations and many are quite affordable, especially with grants and scholarships. Just remember that finding the right fit for you is more important than going to the number one college in anything. These rankings are ephemeral and based on personal opinions. As it does change often, be sure to check the *U.S. News & World Report* site (see www.usnews.com/best-colleges) for updates on this information. You can search the website for colleges by state, by certain degrees, by university type, and more. The Princeton Review website (see www.princetonreview.com) also ranks universities and contains lots of good information about all things college, including advice on taking the ACT and SAT.

THE BEST VALUE FOR YOUR PHYSICAL THERAPY EDUCATION

You should expect to spend about 100–125 additional credit hours pursuing your doctor of physical therapy degree. The total estimated tuition costs vary significantly, but can range from $35,000 to $120,000 or more, depending in part on your resident status. If you are attending a state university and cost is an issue, it makes sense to attend a college in your resident state. Some particularly affordable schools include the following; these assume you attend as a resident of that state:

- University of California, San Francisco (www.ucsf.edu)
- Texas Woman's University (www.twu.edu)
- University of Oklahoma Health Sciences Center (www.ouhsc.edu)
- University of Nebraska Medical Center (www.unmc.edu)
- Virginia Commonwealth University School of Allied Professions (www.vcu.edu)
- University of Illinois College of Applied Health Sciences (www.ahs.illinois.edu)
- University of Wisconsin–Madison (www.wisc.edu)
- University of Colorado Anschutz Medical Campus (www.ucdenver .edu/anschutz)
- University of Kentucky College of Health Sciences (www.uky.edu)
- University of Iowa (www.uiowa.edu)[8]

If your resident state isn't represented here, don't fret too much. This is just a sampling of particularly affordable schools. If cost is an issue, look at some reputable online programs, such as Capella University (www.capella.edu) and Walden University (www.waldenu.edu), as well. (But be careful with for-profit universities; make sure they are on the level. Check their graduation rates as one indicator of student success.)

You can also start your college search in-state with the best school you think you'll be accepted to and apply for scholarships and grants. Financial aid and related financials are covered in more depth later in this chapter.

Finally, don't forget about the physical therapist assistant (PTA) position, which is a growing field and requires only an associate's degree. You can begin working in the field you love much sooner, gain experience, and return to school later to earn the full degree, perhaps with financial help from your employer.

Occupational Therapy: Degree Required and Statistical Data

In order to practice in the United States as an OT, you currently need a master's degree. This typically takes two years to complete after graduating with an applicable undergraduate degree. All states also require OTs to be licensed. Note that by 2025, a doctoral degree will be considered the entry-level education for OTs.

The US BLS[9] reports that the average pay for an OT in 2016 (the most recent data at the time of this writing) was $81,900. The job growth/outlook for the decade 2016–2026 is 24 percent, which is much faster than average. This is universally considered a good, viable, growing field.

GREAT SCHOOLS FOR OCCUPATIONAL THERAPY

There are many different ways to judge something as "great," "the best," and so forth. What might be a great school for you might be too difficult, too expensive, or not rigorous enough for someone else. Keep in mind the advice of the previous sections when deciding what you really need in a school.

As one example of the way things can be ranked, here are some of the top schools for occupational therapy, ranked and compiled in 2016 by *U.S. News & World Report*:

- Boston University, Sargent (www.bu.edu/sargent)
- Washington University in St. Louis (wustl.edu)
- University of Southern California (www.usc.edu)
- University of Illinois (www.uic.edu)
- University of Pittsburgh (www.pitt.edu)
- Colorado State University (www.colostate.edu)
- Thomas Jefferson University (www.jefferson.edu)
- Tufts University (www.tufts.edu)[10]

These rankings are based on peer assessments from other schools' professors, professionals, and deans. Only fully accredited programs in good standing during the survey period were ranked.

These schools represent a fairly diverse sample of geographical locations and many are quite affordable, especially with grants and scholarships. Just remember that finding the right fit for you is more important than going to the number one college in anything. These rankings are ephemeral and based on personal opinions. As it does change often, be sure to check the *U.S. News & World Report* website (see www.usnews.com/best-colleges) for updates on this information. You can search the website for colleges by state, by certain degrees, by university type, and more. The Princeton Review website (see www.princetonreview.com) also ranks universities and contains lots of good information about all things college, including advice on taking the ACT and SAT.

THE BEST VALUE FOR YOUR OCCUPATIONAL THERAPY EDUCATION

The total estimated tuition costs for a master's degree for an OT vary significantly, but can range from $15,000 to $70,000 or more, depending in part on your resident status. If you are attending a state university and cost is an issue, it makes sense to attend a college in your resident state. Some particularly affordable schools include the following; these assume you attend as a resident of that state:

- San José State University, California (www.sjsu.edu)
- Salem State University, Massachusetts (www.salemstate.edu)
- Louisiana State University New Orleans School of Allied Health Professions (www.lsuhsc.edu)

- University of Florida Health (www.ufhealth.edu)
- Towson University, Maryland (www.towson.edu)
- Texas Tech University Health Sciences Center (www.ttuhsc.edu)
- Colorado State University (www.colostate.edu)
- Cleveland State University in Ohio (www.csuohio.edu)

If your resident state isn't represented here, don't fret too much. This is just a sampling of particularly affordable schools. If cost is an issue, look at some reputable online programs, such as Maryville University (www.maryville.edu) and Walden University (www.waldenu.edu), as well. (But be careful with for-profit universities; make sure they are on the level. Check their graduation rates as one indicator of student success.)

You can also start your college search in-state with the best school you think you'll be accepted to and apply for scholarships and grants. Financial aid and related financials are covered in more depth later in this chapter.

Finally, don't forget about the occupational therapist assistant position, which is a growing field and requires only an associate's degree. You can begin working in the field you love much sooner, gain experience, and return to school later to earn the full degree, perhaps with financial help from your employer.

MAKE THE MOST OF CAMPUS VISITS

If it's at all practical and feasible, you should visit the campuses of all the schools you're considering. To get a real feel for any college or university, you need to walk around the campus, spend some time in the common areas where students hang out, and sit in on a few classes. You can also sign up for campus tours, which are typically given by current students. This is another good way to see the campus and ask questions of someone who knows. Be sure to visit the specific school/building that covers your intended major as well. Websites and brochures won't be able to convey that intangible feeling you'll get from a visit.

Make a list of questions that are important to you before you visit. In addition to the questions listed earlier in this chapter, consider these questions as well:

- What is the makeup of the current freshman class? Is the campus diverse?
- What is the meal plan like? What are the food options?

- Where do most of the students hang out between classes? (Be sure to visit this area.)
- How long does it take to walk from one end of campus to the other?
- What types of transportation are available for students? Does campus security provide escorts to cars, dorms, etc., at night?

To prepare for your visit and make the most of it, consider these tips and words of advice:

- Be sure to do some research. At the very least, spend some time on the college's website. You may find your questions are addressed adequately there.
- Make a list of questions.
- Arrange to meet with a professor in your area of interest or to visit the specific school.
- Be prepared to answer questions about yourself and why you are interested in this school.
- Dress in neat, clean, and casual clothes. Avoid overly wrinkled clothing or anything with stains.
- Finally, be sure to send thank-you notes or e-mails after the visit. Remind the recipient when you visited the campus and thank them for their time.

Recreational Therapy: Degree Required and Statistical Data

In order to practice in the United States as a recreational therapist (RT), you currently need an associate's or bachelor's degree. Many employers require their RTs to be certified. To become a certified therapeutic recreation specialist, you must have a bachelor's degree, complete an internship in the field, and then pass an exam.

The US BLS[11] reports that the average pay for an RT in 2016 (the most recent data at the time of this writing) was $46,400. The job growth/outlook for the decade 2016–2026 is 7 percent, which is as fast as average. Evidence shows that job prospects look best for RTs who have a bachelor's degree and the proper certification, and who specialize in working with the elderly, due to the large and growing elderly population.

GREAT SCHOOLS FOR RECREATIONAL THERAPY

There are many different ways to judge something as "great," "the best," and so forth. What might be a great school for you might be too difficult, too expensive, or not rigorous enough for someone else. Keep in mind the advice of the previous sections when deciding what you really need in a school.

Upon graduation, recreational therapy majors must take national and state licensing exams, so be sure you apply only to schools that are recognized by the National Council for Therapeutic Recreation Certification, with curriculum aligned with exam topics and a record of high passing rates. Here are some schools favorably rated for degrees for RTs:

- Alderson Broaddus University (www.ab.edu)
- Ashland University (www.ashland.edu)
- Austin Community College District (www.austincc.edu)
- Benedict College (www.benedict.edu)
- Brigham Young University Provo (www.byu.edu)
- Calvin College (www.calvin.edu)
- Catawba College (www.catawba.edu)
- Central Michigan University (www.cmich.edu)[12]

These schools represent a nice variety of geographical locations and many are quite affordable, especially with grants and scholarships. Remember that finding the right fit for you is more important than going to the number one college in anything. The Princeton Review website (see www.princetonreview .com) also ranks universities and contains lots of good information about all things college, including advice on taking the ACT and SAT.

If cost is an issue, look at some reputable online programs, such as Maryville University (www.maryville.edu) and Walden University (www.waldenu.edu), as well. (But be careful with for-profit universities; make sure they are on the level. Check their graduation rates as one indicator of student success.)

You can also start your college search in-state with the best school you think you'll be accepted to and apply for scholarships and grants. Financial aid and related financials are covered in more depth later in this chapter.

THE BEST VALUE FOR YOUR RECREATIONAL THERAPY EDUCATION

The best value when pursuing an RT degree is to pursue an associate's degree, get your experience in the form of internships or fieldwork, and then hold a job as an RTA. You can later continue schooling and obtain a bachelor's degree while working and your employer will likely pay for at least some of that schooling. This is a longer process, of course, and requires working full-time and going to school, which can be very challenging.

As mentioned in other sections, another important cost consideration is to attend a state school in your state of residence. This will save you as much as 50 percent on your tuition. You can also apply for scholarships and grants. More financial aid and related financials are covered later in this chapter.

Exercise Physiology: Degree Required and Statistical Data

In order to practice in the United States as an exercise physiologist (EP), you need a bachelor's in a related field, such as exercise science, kinesiology, anatomy, physiology, or nutrition. There currently is no national standardized education track that you have to follow to become an EP, but that could certainly change in the near future, given the way the other allied health careers have gone.

Certification requirements vary by state, but are minimal as well. However, to increase your job prospects, it's wise to be certified by the American Society of Exercise Physiologists (ASEP).

The US BLS[13] reports that the average pay for an EP in 2016 (the most recent data at the time of this writing) was $47,340. The job outlook for the decade 2016–2026 is 13 percent, which is faster than average. This is considered a new but growing field.

GREAT SCHOOLS FOR EXERCISE PHYSIOLOGY

Since there is no specific exercise physiology degree, you'll likely be pursuing a degree in exercise science or kinesiology. These are the most common, but there are in fact many degrees that will prepare you for a job in exercise physiology, as discussed in chapter 2. The good news is that this gives you more options in terms of finding good schools. The bad news is that it can make the process a bit more fuzzy in the sense that it's sometimes difficult to determine exactly what employers will expect from you as a new graduate.

Be sure to check out the website of ASEP (see www.asep.org), the certification organization for EPs. In addition to certification information, the website can give you a view of the profession and what employers are looking for.

Here is a listing of schools with great reputations in exercise science and kinesiology:

- George Fox University (www.georgefox.edu)
- Columbia University (www.columbia.edu)
- Rice University (www.rice.edu)
- University of Michigan (www.umich.edu)
- University of Virginia (www.virginia.edu)
- University of North Carolina at Chapel Hill (www.unc.edu)
- University of Southern California (www.usc.edu)
- St. Olaf College (www.wp.stolaf.edu)[14]

These schools represent a nice variety of geographical locations and many are quite affordable, especially with grants and scholarships. Just remember that finding the right fit for you is more important than going to the number one college in anything. The Princeton Review website (see www.princetonreview .com) also ranks universities and contains lots of good information about all things college, including advice on taking the ACT and SAT.

THE BEST VALUE FOR YOUR EXERCISE PHYSIOLOGY EDUCATION

If cost is an issue, look at some reputable online programs as well, such as Post University or Strayer University. (But be careful with for-profit universities; make sure they are on the level. Check their graduation rates as one indicator of student success.)

You can also start your college search in-state with the best school you think you'll be accepted to and apply for scholarships and grants. Financial aid and related financials are covered in more depth later in this chapter.

The total estimated tuition costs for a kinesiology and exercise science major vary significantly, but can range from $15,000 to $37,000 or more per year, depending in part on your resident status. If you are attending a state university and cost is an issue, it makes sense to attend a college in your resident state. For two-year kinesiology and exercise science associate programs, the average total cost per year is $17,070, with an average two-year total program cost of $34,140.[15]

Athletic Training: Degree Required and Statistical Data

In order to practice in the United States as an athletic trainer, you currently need to earn a bachelor's or master's degree from an accredited education program, pass a test administered by the National Athletic Trainers' Association, and pass state licensure exams. According to the NATA, more than 70 percent of ATCs have a master's or even a doctoral degree.

The US BLS[16] reports that the average pay for an athletic trainer in 2016 (the most recent data at the time of this writing) was $45,630. The job outlook for the decade 2016–2026 is 23 percent, which is faster than average. This is considered a stable and viable field.

GREAT SCHOOLS FOR ATHLETIC TRAINING

There are many different ways to judge something as "great," "the best," and so forth. What might be a great school for you might be too difficult, too expensive, or not rigorous enough for someone else. Keep in mind the advice of the previous sections when deciding what you really need in a school.

Here are some schools favorably rated for degrees in athletic training:

- University of Michigan (www.umich.edu)
- University of Florida, Gainesville (www.ufl.edu)
- University of Illinois at Urbana-Champaign (www.illinois.edu)
- University of Texas at Austin (www.utexas.edu)
- Boston University (www.bu.edu)[17]

These schools represent a fairly diverse sample of geographical locations and many are quite affordable, especially with grants and scholarships. Just remember that finding the right fit for you is more important than going to the number one college in anything. In addition, the Princeton Review website (see www.prince tonreview.com) also ranks universities and contains lots of good information about all things college, including advice on taking the ACT and SAT.

THE BEST VALUE FOR YOUR ATHLETIC TRAINER EDUCATION

If cost is an issue, look at some reputable online programs as well such as through Arizona State University online. (But be careful with for-profit universities; make sure they are on the level. Check their graduation rates as one indicator of student success.)

You can also start your college search in-state with the best school you think you'll be accepted to and apply for scholarships and grants. Remember that attending in-state public colleges and universities will save you as much as 50 percent in tuition right off the bat. Financial aid and related financials are covered in more depth later in this chapter.

A PASSION FOR CHANGING LIVES

Sharon Phillips

Sharon Phillips, originally from South Africa, got her first certification related to exercise science in high school when she was sixteen. She moved to the United States to be a nanny when she was a teen and pursued her passion for athletic training through various certifications. She has been a teacher in the physical fitness world for thirty years. She is self-educated and got all her certifications on her own. She worked as a personal trainer for twenty years and now concentrates on group fitness, education, and athletic training, including training the Indianapolis Colts cheerleaders.

Why did you choose to become an athletic trainer?

I think it started in high school for me. I was a competitive athlete, but I didn't go as far as I think I could have if I'd had the right coaching and training. I really enjoy helping to train others to get them stronger and meet their goals; it's so rewarding.

So I really enjoy coaching and training others. I love to train the body, whether it's to be an athlete or to help someone change their lives to be healthy and lose weight. I want people to feel good and for their bodies to be healthy. The state of your body is important to your overall health and happiness. My direction over the years has definitely changed, from a focus on peak athletic performance to concentrating on educating and motivating people to live healthy and active lives.

What is a typical day on the job for you?

I usually teach three classes a day—more than that and it's hard to keep the energy going. It can become too much physically and mentally if you push it. I also do about ninety minutes of my own workout. Once a week, I have one day off where I don't do anything, either teach or my own workouts. That's for mental fitness.

What's the best part of your job?

Changing lives. You are making a difference and making people feel good about themselves. You are helping people with real health challenges, even with issues such as cancer, get better and feel better. It's a huge passion. I also really love the coaching and training in big groups, like the Colts cheerleaders. By the same token, I enjoy attending seminars and conferences and training and educating other professionals in the field. Training the trainers, so to speak.

What's the worst or most challenging part of your job?

The lack of buy-in sometimes—people don't do what they know they need to. Whether it's the change in eating habits or the steady exercise regimen, you try to motive people, but they have to decide to make the changes. I see clearly that poor eating and lack of exercise in our society is killing people. However, this is both a challenge for me and a real reward when I can help people make changes and feel so much better. It takes time and kindness to convince people sometimes that they can lead a healthier life.

What's the most surprising thing about your job?

The industry changes every day—issues around fat, cancer, carbs, etc. It's a real challenge to keep up and figure out what's real and what's a fad.

What kinds of qualities do you think one needs to be successful at this job?

First of all, get educated in exercise science and human movement. My path was a different one and I feel good about where I'm at, but it's a regret of mine that I never got a degree. Get your credentials, including from the National Academy of Sports Medicine, [American College of Sports Medicine], ACE [American Council on Exercise], and AFAA [Aerobics and Fitness Association of America].

I can't stress enough that sincerity, passion, and kindness are all very important. You need to be gentle and kind to people who don't exercise and have an issue with their bodies and a block about feeling good. You have to get the mind before you get the body. You should be motivated by wanting to make a difference, because you might have to put in years before you can really make a good living. Trust and rapport take time to build.

You must be a people person, be motivated, and be a cheerleader. Finally, don't count out the aspect of this job that's psychological coaching. It's a mind-set and it's often affected by the chemicals in the foods we eat.

How do you combat burnout?

It's important to listen to your body and take recovery days yourself. Make sure you are living the lifestyle that you're promoting. I find that learning new things and continuing to learn from others keeps me interested and excited.

What would you tell a young person who is thinking about becoming a trainer?

If you think you're the best at everything, you will go nowhere. You must be able to take feedback and use it. Take certifications and keep getting educated. Be open for feedback.

It's a good career for family-oriented people, as it's hourly and you can pick your own hours. It's flexible but not a huge moneymaking career.

Remember, to change a life, you have to be sincere about it.

Your Massage Therapy Degree Plan

You can enter massage therapy school directly after graduating from high school or receiving your general equivalency diploma (GED). This involves a relatively short educational experience (about nine months to two years, depending on the state and the intensity of your study). You don't need a college degree to practice, but like many professions, it's smart—and often required, depending on the state—to pursue continuing education each year, perhaps by learning a new modality, for example.

To practice as a massage therapist, you also need to earn a certificate or license in massage therapy, which typically involves 500–1,000 hours of academic and clinical work. The magic number of hours required varies by state, although the American Massage Therapy Association (AMTA) recommends a minimum of 500 hours of training.[18] Some states require certification and some require licensing (usually a more stringent process). The licensing process typically involves sitting for an exam, most often the Massage and Bodywork Licensing Exam (MBLEx).[19]

In addition to your state's requirements, you can also become board certified in massage therapy. The board certification is awarded through a test by the National Certification Board for Therapeutic Massage and Bodywork (NCBTMB; see www.ncbtmb.org). Board certification shows that you have the skills, abilities, knowledge and attributes to practice, as determined by the NCBTMB.

Finding a school or program near you that offers massage therapy degrees is usually not a problem, but be sure you pick a reputable one that is recognized by your state's licensing board. One way of knowing whether a training program or massage school provides a nationally recognized standard level of education is to see if it is accredited by a credible agency, that is, one that follows the guidelines of the US Department of Education.

As a starting place, visit MassageTherapy.org (www.massagetherapylicense .org), which is state-by-state listing of requirements for licensing, education, and certification of massage therapists. This site has a clickable map and alphabetical listing of states, and with a single click you can easily find any state's requirements. This site also has good articles about finding a school and employment-related articles for massage therapists.

STATISTICAL DATA

The US BLS[20] reports that the average pay for a massage therapist in 2016 (the most recent data at the time of this writing) was $39,860. The job growth/outlook for the decade 2016–2026 is 26 percent, which is much faster than average. Being certified or licensed and passing professional exams will improve your job prospects, as will being knowledgeable in multiple modalities of massage. When you are new at massage therapy, it does take some time to build your client base.

LIST OF MODALITIES BASED ON DEMAND

To have a healthy and marketable career as a massage therapist, it's important to be trained in as many modalities as you can. The most popular modalities at this time, in order, are Swedish, aromatherapy, hot stone, deep-tissue, Shiatsu, Thai, prenatal, and reflexology. An up-and-coming technique called ortho-bionomy has also gained traction. These are the general current trends and are bound to change over time, so make sure you know what's popular in the area where you live.

The more well-rounded you are in this regard, the more marketable you'll seem to a company looking to hire you and the easier it will be to build your client base. When you look for a good massage school be sure to ask which modalities it is certified to teach to its students.

Financial Aid

Finding the money to attend school—whether a two- or four-year college program, an online program, or a vocational career college—can seem overwhelming. But you can do it if you have a plan before you actually start applying to colleges. If you get into your top-choice university, don't let the sticker price turn you away. Financial aid can come from many different sources, and it's available to cover all different kinds of costs you'll encounter during your years in college, including tuition, fees, books, housing, and food.

Paying for college can take a creative mix of grants, scholarships, and loans,
but you can find your way with some help.

The good news is that universities more often offer incentive or tuition
discount aid to encourage students to attend. The market is often more competitive in the favor of the student, and colleges and universities are responding
by offering more generous aid packages to a wider range of students than they
used to. Here are some basic tips and pointers about the financial aid process:

- Apply for financial aid during your senior year. You must fill out the
  Free Application for Federal Student Aid (FAFSA) form, which can be
  filed starting October 1 of your senior year until June of the year you
  graduate.[21] Because the amount of available aid is limited, it's best to
  apply as soon as you possibly can. See fafsa.gov to get started.
- Be sure to compare and contrast the deals you get from different schools.
  There is room to negotiate with universities. The first offer for aid may
  not be the best you'll get.
- Wait until you receive all offers from your top schools and then use this
  information to negotiate with your top choice to see if they will match
  or beat the best aid package you received.

- To be eligible to keep and maintain your financial aid package, you must meet certain grade/GPA requirements. Be sure you are very clear on these academic expectations and keep up with them.
- You must reapply for federal aid every year.

Watch out for scholarship scams! You should never be asked to pay to submit the FAFSA form (*free* is in its name) or be required to pay a lot to find appropriate aid and scholarships. These are free services. If an organization promises you you'll get aid or that you have to "act now or miss out," these are both warning signs of a less-than-reputable organization.

You should also be careful with your personal information to avoid identity theft as well. Simple things like closing and exiting your browser after visiting sites where you entered personal information go a long way. Don't share your student aid ID number with anyone, either.

It's important to understand the different forms of financial aid that are available to you. That way, you'll know how to apply for different kinds and get the best financial aid package that fits your needs and strengths. The two main categories that financial aid falls under is gift aid, which don't have to be repaid, and self-help aid, which includes loans that must be repaid and work-study funds that are earned. The next sections cover the various types of financial aid that fit into these areas.

GRANTS

Grants typically are awarded to students who have financial need, but can also be used in the areas of athletics, academics, demographics, veteran support, and special talents. They do not have to be paid back. Grants can come from federal agencies, state agencies, specific universities, and private organizations. Most federal and state grants are based on financial need.

Examples of grants are the Pell Grant, SMART Grant, and the Federal Supplemental Educational Opportunity Grant (FSEOG). Visit the US Department of Education's Federal Student Aid site at studentaid.ed.gov/types/grants-scholarships for lots of current information about grants.

SCHOLARSHIPS

Scholarships are merit-based aid that does not have to be paid back. They are typically awarded based on academic excellence or some other special talent, such as music or art. Scholarships can also be athletic-based, minority-based, aid for women, and so forth. These are typically not awarded by federal or state governments, but instead come from the specific university you applied to as well as private and nonprofit organizations.

Be sure to reach out directly to the financial aid officers of the schools you want to attend. These people are great contacts that can lead you to many more sources of scholarships and financial aid. Visit GoCollege's Financial Aid Finder at www.gocollege.com/financial-aid/scholarships/types for lots more information about how scholarships in general work.

LOANS

Many types of loans are available especially for students to pay for their post-secondary education. However, the important thing to remember here is that loans must be paid back, with interest. (This is the extra cost of borrowing the money and is usually a percentage of the amount you borrow.) Be sure you understand the interest rate you will be charged. Is this fixed or will it change over time? Are payments on the loan and interest deferred until you graduate (meaning you don't have to begin paying it off until after you graduate)? Is the loan subsidized (meaning the federal government pays the interest until you graduate)? These are all points you need to be clear about before you sign on the dotted line.

There are many types of loans offered to students, including need-based loans, non-need-based loans, state loans, and private loans. Two very reputable federal loans are the Perkins Loan and the Direct Stafford Loan. For more information about student loans, visit bigfuture.collegeboard.org/pay-for-college/loans/types-of-college-loans.

FEDERAL WORK-STUDY

The US federal work-study program provides part-time jobs for undergraduate and graduate students with financial need so they can earn money to pay for educational expenses. The focus of such work is on community service and work related to a student's course of study. Not all colleges and universities participate in this program, so be sure to check with the financial aid office at any schools you are considering if this is something you are counting on. The sooner you apply, the more likely you will get the job you desire and be able to benefit from the program, as funds are limited. See studentaid.ed.gov/sa/types/work-study for more information about this opportunity.

Making High School Count

If you are still in high school or middle school, there are still many things you can do now to help the postsecondary educational process go more smoothly. Consider these tips for your remaining years:

- Work on listening well and speaking and communicating clearly. Work on writing clearly and effectively.
- Learn how to learn. This means keeping an open mind, asking questions, asking for help when you need it, taking good notes, and doing your homework.
- Plan a daily homework schedule and keep up with it. Have a consistent, quiet place to study.
- Talk about your career interests with friends, family, and counselors. They may have connections to people in your community who you can shadow or who will mentor you.
- Try new interests and activities, especially during your first two years of high school.
- Be involved in extracurricular activities that truly interest you and say something about who you are and want to be.

Kids are under so much pressure these days to do it all, but you should think about working smarter rather than harder. If you are involved in things you enjoy, your educational load won't seem like such a burden. Be sure to take time for self-care, such as sleep, unscheduled down time, and activities that you find fun and energizing. See chapter 4 for more ways to relieve and avoid stress.

Summary

This chapter looked at all the aspects of college and postsecondary schooling that you'll want to consider as you move forward. Remember that finding the right fit is especially important, as it increases the chances that you'll stay in school and finish your degree—and have an amazing experience while you're there. The six careers covered in this book have varying educational requirements, which means that finding the right school can be very different depending on your career aspirations.

In this chapter, you learned about the great schools out there and how to get the best education for the best deal. You also learned a little about scholarships and financial aid, how the SAT and ACT tests work, and how to write a unique personal statement that eloquently expresses your passions.

Use this chapter as a jumping-off point to dig deeper into your particular area of interest, but don't forget these important points:

- Take the SAT and ACT tests early in your junior year so you have time to take them again. Most universities automatically accept the highest scores.
- Make sure that the institution you plan to attend has an accredited program in your field of study. This is particularly important in the allied health fields. Some professions follow national accreditation policies, while others are state-mandated and therefore differ across state lines. Do your research and understand the differences.
- Don't underestimate how important campus visits are, especially in the pursuit of finding the right academic fit. Come prepared to ask questions not addressed on the school's website or in the literature.
- Your personal statement is a very important piece of your application that can set you apart from other applicants. Take the time and energy needed to make it unique and compelling.
- Don't assume you can't afford a school based on the sticker price. Many schools offer great scholarships and aid to qualified students. It doesn't hurt to apply. This advice especially applies to minorities, veterans, and students with disabilities.
- Several of the education-heavy professions (such as occupational therapy and physical therapy) have related assistant positions that require only

an associate's degree. This can be a way to start working sooner and have your employer pay for continuing education.

- Don't lose sight of the fact that it's important to pursue a career that you enjoy, are good at, and are passionate about! You'll be a happier person if you do so.

At this point, your career goals and aspirations should be jelling. At the least, you should have a plan for finding out more information. And don't forget about networking, which was covered in more detail in chapter 2. Remember to do research about the university, school, or degree program before you reach out and especially before you visit. Faculty and staff find students who ask challenging questions much more impressive than those who ask questions that can be answered by spending ten minutes on the school's website.

Chapter 4 goes into detail about the next steps—writing a résumé and cover letter, interviewing well, follow-up communication, and more. This information is not just for college grads; you can use it to secure internships, volunteer positions, summer jobs, and other opportunities. In fact, the sooner you can hone these communication skills, the better off you'll be in the professional world.

Writing Your Résumé and Interviewing

No matter which path you decide to take—whether you enter the workforce immediately after high school, go to college first and then look for a job, or maybe do something in between, having a well-written résumé and stellar interviewing skills will help you reach your ultimate goals. This chapter provides some helpful tips and advice to build the best résumé and cover letter, how to interview well with prospective employers, and how to communicate effectively and professionally at all times. The advice in this chapter isn't just for would-be professionals, either; it can help you score that internship or summer job or help you give a great college interview to impress the admissions office.

After discussing how to write your résumé, the chapter looks at important interviewing skills that you can build and develop over time. The chapter also has some tips for dealing successfully with stress, which is an inevitable by-product of a busy life.

Writing Your Résumé

If you're a teen writing a résumé for your first job, you likely don't have a lot of work experience under your belt yet. Because of this limited work experience, you need to include classes and coursework that are related to the job you're seeking, as well as any school activities and volunteer experience you have. While you are writing your résumé, you might discover some talents and recall some activities that you forgot about, which are important to add. Think about volunteer work, side jobs you've held (babysitting, dog walking, etc.), and the like. A good approach at this point in your career is to build a functional résumé, which focuses on your abilities rather than work experience, and it's discussed in detail next.

PARTS OF A RÉSUMÉ

The functional résumé is the best approach when you don't have a lot of pertinent work experience, as it is written to highlight your abilities rather than your experience. (The other, perhaps more common, type of résumé is the chronological résumé, which lists a person's accomplishments in chronological order, most recent jobs listed first.) This section breaks down and discusses the functional résumé in greater detail.

Here are the essential parts of your résumé, listed from the top down:

- *Heading:* This should include your name, address, and contact information, including phone, e-mail, and website if you have one. This information is typically centered at the top of the page.
- *Objective:* This is a one-sentence statement that tells the employer what kind of position you are seeking. This should be modified to be specific to each potential employer.
- *Education:* Always list your most recent school or program first. Include date of completion (or expected date of graduation), degree or certificate earned, and the institution's name and address. Include workshops, seminars, and related classes here as well.
- *Skills:* Skills include computer literacy, leadership skills, organizational skills, and time-management skills. Be specific in this area when possible.
- *Activities:* Activities can be related to skills. Perhaps an activity listed here led to you developing a skill listed above. This section can be combined with the Skills section, but it's often helpful to break these apart if you have enough substantive things to say in both areas. Examples include sports teams, leadership roles, community service work, clubs and organizations, and so on.
- *Experience:* If you don't have any actual work experience that's relevant, you might consider skipping this section. However, you can list summer, part-time, and volunteer jobs you've held.
- *Interests:* This section is optional, but it's a chance to include special talents and interests. Keep it short, factual, and specific.
- *References:* It's best to say that references are available on request. If you do list actual contacts, list no more than three and make sure you inform your contacts that they might be contacted.

The first three parts are pretty much standard, but the others can be creatively combined or developed to maximize your abilities and experience. These are not set-in-stone sections that every résumé must have. As an example, consider this mock functional résumé.

Henry James Smith

628 Main Street
Portland, OR, 97035
Phone: 503-503-5030 E-Mail: henrythecat@henry.com

Objective

Seeking an entry-level position in the health care industry to further my passion and desire to work with the elderly

Education

High School Diploma, June 2018
Westhaven High School, Portland, OR
GPA: 3.87. Top 4% of class

Skills

Computer literacy on PC and Mac; MS Word, Excel, PowerPoint, desktop publishing, web software
Trained in first aid and CPR
Four years of Spanish

Activities

Captain of the Spanish Club, 2018
Outstanding Community Service Award, 2017

Experience

2017 internship co-op participant, Standport Health & Living Long-Term Care Facility, Portland OR
June 2016-June 2017, Part-time volunteer, Primelife Senior Center, Portland, OR
May 2015-June 2016, Crew Team Member, Big Burger Stop 'N Eat, Portland, OR

References

Available upon request

A functional-style résumé is a good template to use when you don't have a lot of work experience.

If you're still not seeing the big picture here, it's helpful to look at student and part-time résumé examples online to see how others have approached this process. Search for "functional résumé examples" to get a look at some examples.

RÉSUMÉ-WRITING TIPS

Regardless of your situation and why you're writing the résumé, there are some basic tips and techniques you should use:

- Keep it short and simple. This includes using a simple, standard font and format. Using one of the résumé templates included in your word processor software can be a great way to start.
- Use simple language. Keep it to one page.
- Highlight your academic achievements, such as a high GPA (above 3.5) or academic awards. If you have taken classes related to the job you're interviewing for, list those briefly as well.
- Emphasize your extracurricular activities, internships, and the like. These could include clubs, sports, dog walking, babysitting, or volunteer work. Use these activities to show your skills and abilities.
- Use action verbs, such as *led, created, taught, ran,* and *developed.*
- Be specific and give examples.
- Always be honest.
- Include leadership roles and experience.
- Edit and proofread at least twice, and have someone else do the same. Ask a professional (such as your school writing center or your local library services) to proofread it for you also. Don't forget to run spell check.
- Include a cover letter (discussed in the next section).

THE COVER LETTER

Every résumé you send out should include a cover letter. This can be the most important part of your job search because it's often the first thing that potential employers read. By including the cover letter, you're showing the employers that you took the time to learn about their organization and address them personally. This goes a long way to show that you're interested in the position.

Henry James Smith
628 Main Street
Portland, OR 97035

Ms. Sylvia Gonzalez
Director of Human Resources
Henaryne Healthcare
974 N. Franklin
Portland, OR 97035

Dear Ms. Gonzalez,

I'm writing based on the article I read in the October 9th edition of the *Portland Star*. In the article, you were quoted as saying "we need more skilled intake personnel to effectively serve the growing Spanish-speaking population" around your facility.

I believe my experience with both the Spanish language and with local healthcare facilities can help address the need you have with Henaryne Healthcare. I have four years of Spanish experience, and I can speak near fluently. For the past two years, I've served as a part-time tutor for students who know English as a second language (ESL). This has helped me improve my Spanish and given me terrific interpersonal skills.

I'm ready to use my Spanish skills in the healthcare environment, which is my career goal. I've had several internships and cooperative experiences in local healthcare, including senior living centers, where I worked with both patients and their families. I'm very good at understanding the needs of others and communicating them to healthcare workers. My computer experience will be a great help in the data entry required of every intake worker.

I'm eager to put my skills to work in your organization, because all parties will benefit from my experience. I look forward to hearing from you at your convenience.

Sincerely,

Henry J. Smith

Henry J. Smith

Your cover letter can be the most important part of your job search because it's often the first thing potential employers see.

Be sure to call the company or verify on the website the name and title of the person to whom you should address the letter. This letter should be brief. Introduce yourself and begin with a statement that will grab the person's attention. Keep in mind that employers potentially receive hundreds of résumés and cover letters for every open position. You want yours to stand out. Important information to include in the cover letter, from the top, includes:

- The current date
- Your address and contact information
- The person's name, company, and contact information

Then you begin the letter portion of the cover letter, which should mention how you heard about the position, something extra about you that will interest the potential employer, practical skills you can bring to the position, and past experience related to the job. You should apply the facts outlined in your résumé to the job to which you're applying. Each cover letter should be personalized for the position and company to which you're applying. Don't use "To whom it may concern"; instead, take the time to find out to whom you should actually address the letter. Finally, end with a complimentary closing, such as "Sincerely, Henry Smith" and be sure to add your signature. Search for "sample cover letters for internships" or "sample cover letters for high schoolers" to see some good examples. Consider this mock cover letter as an example.

If you are e-mailing your cover letter instead of printing it out, you'll need to pay particular attention to the subject line of your e-mail. Be sure that it is specific to the position you are applying for. In all cases, it's really important to follow the employer's instructions about how to submit your cover letter and résumé.

EFFECTIVELY HANDLING STRESS

As you're forging ahead with your life plans—whether it's college, a full-time job, or even a gap year—you might find that these decisions feel very important and heavy and that the stress is difficult to deal with. This is completely normal. Try these simple techniques to relieve stress:

- Take deep breaths in and out. Try this for thirty seconds. You'll be amazed at how it can help.
- Close your eyes and clear your mind.
- Go scream at the passing subway car. Or lock yourself in a closet and scream. Or scream into a pillow. For some people, this can really help.
- Keep the issue in perspective. Any decision you make now can be changed if it doesn't work out.

Want to know how to avoid stress altogether? It is surprisingly simple. Of course, simple doesn't always mean easy, but these ideas are basic and make sense based on what we know about the human body:

- Get enough sleep.
- Eat healthy.
- Get exercise.
- Go outside.
- Schedule downtime.
- Connect with friends and family.

The bottom line is that you need to take time for self-care. There will always be stress, but how you deal with it makes all the difference. This only becomes more important as you enter college or the workforce and maybe have a family. Developing good, consistent habits related to self-care now will serve you all your life.

"It's important to listen to your body and take recovery days yourself. Make sure you are living the lifestyle that you're promoting. I find that learning new things and continuing to learn from others keeps me interested and excited."—Sharon Phillips, athletic trainer

Interviewing Skills

The best way to avoid nerves and keep calm when you're interviewing is to be prepared. It's okay to feel scared, but keep it in perspective. It's likely that you'll receive many more rejections than acceptances in your professional life, as we all do. However, you only need one *yes* to start out. Think of the interviewing process as a learning experience. With the right attitude, you will learn from each one and get better with each subsequent interview. That should be your overarching goal. Consider these tips and tricks when interviewing, whether it be for a job, internship, college admission, or something else entirely:

- Practice interviewing with a friend or relative. Practicing will help calm your nerves and make you feel more prepared. Ask for specific feedback.

Do you need to speak more loudly? Are you making enough eye contact? Are you actively listening when the other person is speaking?

- Learn as much as you can about the company, school, or organization, and be sure to understand the position for which you're applying. This will show the interviewer that you are motivated and interested in the organization.
- Speak up during the interview. Convey to the interviewer important points about you. Don't be afraid to ask questions. Try to remember the interviewers' names and call them by name.
- Arrive early and dress professionally and appropriately. (You can read more about proper dress in a following section.)
- Take some time to prepare answers to commonly asked questions. Be ready to describe your career or educational goals to the interviewer.[1]

Common questions you may be asked during a job interview include:

- Tell me about yourself.
- What are your greatest strengths?
- What are your weaknesses?
- Tell me something about yourself that's not on your résumé.
- What are your career goals?
- How do you handle failure? Are you willing to fail?
- How do you handle stress and pressure?
- What are you passionate about?
- Why do you want to work for us?

Common questions you may be asked during a college admissions interview include:

- Tell me about yourself.
- Why are you interested in going to college?
- Why do you want to major in this subject?
- What are your academic strengths?
- What are your academic weaknesses? How have you addressed them?
- What will you contribute to this college/school/university?
- Where do you see yourself in ten years?
- How do you handle failure? Are you willing to fail?

- How do you handle stress and pressure?
- Whom do you most admire?
- What is your favorite book?
- What do you do for fun?
- Why are you interested in this college/school/university?

Jot down notes about your answers to these questions, but don't try to memorize the answers. You don't want to come off as too rehearsed during the interview. Remember to be as specific and detailed as possible when answering these questions. Your goal is to set yourself apart in some way from the other interviewees. Always accentuate the positive, even when you're asked about something you did not like, or about failure or stress. Most importantly, though, be yourself.

Active listening is the process of fully concentrating on what is being said, understanding it, and providing nonverbal cues and responses to the person talking.[2] It's the opposite of being distracted and thinking about something else when someone is talking. Active listening takes practice. You might find that your mind wanders and you need to bring it back to the person talking (and this could happen multiple times during one conversation). Practice this technique in regular conversations with friends and relatives. In addition to giving a better interview, it can cut down on nerves and make you more popular with friends and family, as everyone wants to feel that they are really being heard. For more on active listening, check out www.mindtools.com/CommSkll/ActiveListening.htm.

You should also be ready to ask questions of your interviewer. In a practical sense, there should be some questions you have that you can't find the answer to on the website or in the literature. Also, asking questions shows that you are interested and have done your homework. Avoid asking questions about salary, scholarships, or special benefits at this stage, and don't ask about anything negative you've heard about the company or school. Keep the questions positive and related to the position to which you're applying. Some example questions to potential employers include:

- What is a typical career path for a person in this position?
- How would you describe the ideal candidate for this position?
- How is the department organized?
- What kind of responsibilities come with this job? (Don't ask this if they've already addressed this question in the job description or discussion.)
- What can I do as a follow-up?
- When do you expect to reach a decision?

See "Make the Most of Campus Visits" in chapter 3 for some good examples of questions to ask the college admissions office. The important thing is to write your own questions related to information you really want to know. This will show genuine interest.

Dressing Appropriately

It's important to determine what is actually appropriate in the setting of the interview. What is appropriate in a corporate setting might be different from what you'd expect at a small liberal arts college or at a large hospital setting.

Even something like "business casual" can be interpreted in many ways,
so do some research to find out what exactly is expected of you.

For example, most college admissions offices suggest business casual attire, but depending on the job interview, you may want to step it up from there. Again, it's important to do your homework and be prepared. In addition to reading up on the organization's guidelines, it never hurts to take a look around the website if you can see what other people are wearing to work or to interviews. Regardless of the setting, make sure your clothes are not wrinkled, untidy, or stained. Avoid flashy clothing of any kind.

Follow-Up Communication

Be sure to follow up, whether via e-mail or via regular mail, with a thank-you note to the interviewer. This is appropriate whether you're interviewing for a job or internship or with a college. In addition to showing consideration, it will trigger the interviewer's memory about you and show that you have genuine interest in the position, company, or school. Be sure to follow the business letter format and highlight the key points of your interview and experience at the company or university.

What Employers Expect

Regardless of the job, profession, or field you end up working in, there are universal characteristics that all employers—and schools, for that matter look for in candidates. At this early stage in your professional life, you have an opportunity to recognize which of these foundational characteristics are your strengths (and therefore highlight them in an interview) and which are weaknesses (and therefore continue to work on them and build them up). Consider these characteristics:

- Positive attitude
- Dependability
- Desire to continue to learn
- Initiative
- Effective communication
- Cooperation
- Organization

This is not an exhaustive list, and other characteristics can very well include things like sensitivity to others, honesty, good judgment, loyalty, responsibility, and punctuality. Specific to the allied health careers, you can add empathy, flexibility, attention to detail, and physical fitness to that list. Consider these important characteristics when you answer the common questions that employers ask. It pays to work these traits into the answers—of course, being honest and realistic about your traits.

Beware the social media trap! Prospective employers and colleges will check your social media profile, so make sure there is nothing too personal, explicit, or inappropriate out there. When you communicate with the world on social media, don't use profanity—and be sure to use proper grammar. Think about the version of yourself you are portraying online. Is it favorable or at least neutral to potential employers? They will look, rest assured.

LEARN HOW TO MARKET YOURSELF

Jeff Thomas

Jeff Thomas is a trainer and group training coordinator for a large national health and fitness company. He has been in the industry for twelve years, starting off at Nike as a master basketball trainer.

What is a typical day on the job for you?

Since you need to adhere to your clients' needs and wishes, the schedule can be somewhat variable. Whatever works best for your clients is what you need to do. Hours are variable and you don't always have a typical day. Often you work very early before the normal workday and then after the workday is over, because that's when people can come in for training.

There are set shifts where I work, which are either 6:00 a.m. to 2:00 p.m. or 12:00 p.m. to 8:00 p.m. Since the job is 100 percent commission, it's best to not limit yourself to certain hours. You need to be out there getting in front of people.

As a group training coordinator, my typical day begins by looking at how the group training program is going, including revenue numbers, and helping my instructors as much as I can. I have one-on-one coaching and group meetings with the trainers to help guide them and help them meet their goals.

In terms of the training I do with clients, it can be one-on-one training, teaching classes, or even two-on-one sessions. In any case, I always help the client determine their goals first, depending on what they want to achieve.

How do you build your client base?

I used the group programs to find clients when I first started. I get as many people in front of me as I can. You have to build your business by programming and networking. You can reach out to new members of the club as well. You are as busy as you want to be once you build your core base. It's about making relationships. There is no instant business, though—you have to work at it.

What's the worst part of your job?

I think it's the admin—going over business, looking at numbers, and filling out forms.

What is the best part of your job?

The success stories! You help people get down to a certain weight or turn their health issues around, and they change their lives in a positive way and can do things they weren't able to do before. Or you help someone recover from an accident, or help them have a healthy pregnancy. Often these people turn into family friends.

What's the most surprising thing about your job?

How much continuing education helps out your personal growth and the programming you can offer. It's important to keep up with the research.

What's next; where do you see yourself going from here?

I really like my group training coordinator role that I have right now. I get to help other trainers with their business and strategies. So I get to manage and train, which is a nice combination. I enjoy helping out other trainers with tips and education.

Did your education prepare you for the job?

Yes, absolutely. It's important to know what the body does and how it works, the mechanics of the body, including kinesiology. The clinical internships are very helpful as well. Getting that on-the-job experience and training is also invaluable.

How do you combat burnout?

I don't find it to be an issue, but it is important to take time off. Take a vacation or meditate. Maintain your own health and fitness.

What would you tell a young person who is thinking about pursuing this career?

Learn how to market yourself. Don't be afraid of failure. Learn from any *no* and practice your skill. Public speaking is a fear for most people—practice it. Find a good mentor and pick their brain. I had two excellent ones, both of whom really helped further my career.

Personal contacts can make the difference! Don't be afraid to contact people you know. Personal connections can be a great way to find jobs and internship opportunities. Your high school teachers, your coaches and mentors, and your friends' parents are all examples of people who very well may know about jobs or internships that would suit you. Start asking several months before you hope to start a job or internship, because it will take some time to do research and arrange interviews. You can also use social media in your search. LinkedIn (www.linkedin.com), for example, includes lots of searchable information on local companies. Follow and interact with people on social media to get their attention. Just remember to act professionally and communicate with proper grammar, just as you would in person.

Summary

Well, you made it to the end of this book! Hopefully you have learned enough about the allied health field careers featured here to start your journey, or to continue along your path. If you've reach the end and you feel like one of these careers is right for you, that's great news. If you've figured out that this isn't the right field for you, that's good information to learn, too. For many of us, figuring out what we *don't* want to do and what we *don't* like is an important step in finding the right career.

There is a lot of good news about the allied health field, and it's a very smart career choice for anyone with a passion to help people. It's a great career for people who get energy from working with other people and who want to help others live their fullest lives. Job demand is high and there continues to be a shortage of people entering the workforce in all these areas. Whether you decide to attend a four-year university, go to graduate school, go to community college, or take a gap year, having a plan and an idea about your future can help guide your decisions. After reading this book, you should be well on your way to having a plan for your future. Good luck to you as you move ahead!

Glossary

accreditation: The act of officially recognizing an organizational body, person, or educational facility as having a particular status or being qualified to perform a particular activity.

ACT: One of the standardized college entrance tests that anyone wanting to enter undergraduate studies in the United States should take. It measures knowledge and skills in mathematics, English, reading, and science reasoning, as they apply to college readiness. There are four multiple-choice sections and an optional writing test. The total score of the ACT is 36. *See also* SAT.

active listening: The process of fully concentrating on what is being said, understanding it, and providing nonverbal cues and responses to the person talking. It's the opposite of being distracted and thinking about something else when someone is talking to you.

allied health professions: Jobs involving trained health professionals who are not doctors, dentists, or nurses. This is a large area and includes the six professions covered in this book, as well as speech therapists, nutritionists, emergency medical technicians and paramedics, and medical assistants, to name a few. People in these professions provide services pertaining to the diagnosis, evaluation, and prevention of diseases and disorders.

associate's degree: A degree awarded by a community or junior college that typically requires two years of study.

athletic training/trainer: A professional who specializes in preventing, diagnosing, and treating muscle and bone injuries and illnesses that occur due to athletic activities. Athletic trainers usually develop and enact conditioning and training plans and provide first aid, acute care, and rehabilitation to players.

baby boomers: The American generation that was born immediately after World War II, from about 1945 until about 1964. During this time, there was a "boom" (large increase) in the number of births in the United States. This matters to professionals in allied health because as baby boomers continue to age, they will disproportionately need care and services that allied health professionals provide.

bachelor's degree: An undergraduate degree awarded by colleges and universities that is typically a four-year course of study when pursued full-time, but this can vary by the degree earned and by the university awarding the degree.

cardiovascular system: The system of the human body comprising the heart and blood, including veins and arteries. Applicable diseases include stroke, heart attack, and high blood pressure.

cupping: A specialized form of massage whereby the therapist applies special cups to the skin to create suction in areas that are inflamed, have poor blood flow, and are in pain. It is an ancient form of alternative Chinese medicine that dates back thousands of years.

diagnosis: When a healthcare professional determines the nature of an illness or problem after examining a patient.

doctor of physical therapy (DPT) degree: The current standard required to practice as a physical therapist, this degree typically takes three years to complete, usually translating into 109–113 credit hours of graduate coursework. That's three additional years after graduating with an undergraduate degree in something like human biology or anatomy, kinesiology, exercise science, or athletic training.

doctoral degree: The highest level of degree awarded by colleges and universities. This degree qualifies the holder to teach at the university level and requires (usually published) research in the field. Earning a doctoral degree typically requires an additional three to five years of study after earning a bachelor's degree. Anyone with a doctoral degree—not just medical doctors—can be addressed as "Doctor."

endocrine (hormonal) system: The system comprising all kinds of glands in the human body that release various kinds of hormones into the blood. These include the thyroid, adrenal, and testes and ovary glands. Diseases applicable to allied health include diabetes and thyroid disease.

exercise physiologist (EP): A trained physical therapist who analyzes a person's medical history and current level of fitness in order to develop the best exercise and fitness routine for the individual's needs and health status. A bachelor's degree in exercise science, kinesiology, anatomy, physiology, nutrition, or a related area is considered an entry-level requirement to be an EP.

gap year: A gap year is a year between high school and college (or sometimes between college and postgraduate studies) during which the student is not in school but is instead involved in other pursuits, typically a volunteer program such as the Peace Corps, travel, or work and teaching.

gerontology: The study of old age.

grants: Money to pay for postsecondary education that is typically awarded to students who have financial need, but can also be used in the areas of athletics, academics, demographics, veteran support, and special talents. Grants do not have to be paid back.

hydrotherapy: The use of water—including steam, swimming pools, hot tubs, ice baths, etc.—to treat illness and relieve pain and discomfort.

kinesiology: The study of how the body moves and the mechanics of its movement.

master's degree: A postgraduate degree awarded by colleges and universities that requires at least one additional year of study after obtaining a bachelor's degree. The degree holder shows mastery of a specific field.

message therapy: The process of using touch and pressure to manipulate muscles and other soft tissues of the body in order to relieve pain, reduce stress, and increase relaxation. Modalities include Swedish, deep-tissue, infant, and prenatal.

modality: A particular type or category of a field. For example, Swedish massage is a modality of massage therapy.

musculoskeletal system: The bones and smooth tissue muscles of the body, which are involved in humans' movement. Arthritis is an example of a disease of the musculoskeletal system.

myofascial pain syndrome: A disorder in which pressure on sensitive points in the muscles causes pain in what seem like unrelated body parts. This sometimes happens after recurring injuries or muscle overuse. Symptoms include chronic pain or a tender muscle knot.

neuromuscular system: The muscles and nerves in the human body. Diseases related to this system include multiple sclerosis and muscular dystrophy.

occupational therapy: A specialized form of therapy for people recuperating from or managing physical or mental illnesses, with the goal of helping them best perform their daily "occupations," whether that be as a student, a retiree, or other.

ortho-bionomy: A gentle, noninvasive method of massage that's been shown to be effective at relieving stress and injuries related to a physical imbalance or improper posture issues.

personal statement: A written description of your accomplishments, outlook, interest, goals, and personality that is an important part of your college application. The personal statement should set you apart from other applicants. The required length depends on the institution, but they generally range from one to two pages, or 500–1,000 words.

physical therapy: The process of using actual movements (sometimes called biomechanics or kinesiology), exercise therapy, and manual (hands-on) therapy to improve a person's physical impairment and reduce any related pain.

physiotherapy/physiotherapist: The name for the profession of physical therapy outside of the United States.

postsecondary degree: An educational degree above and beyond a high school education. This is a general description that includes trade certificates and certifications; associate's, bachelor's, master's degrees; and beyond.

pulmonary system: The specific part of the respiratory system that carries deoxygenated blood away from the heart into the lungs to be oxygenated again. Diseases of the pulmonary system include asthma and chronic obstructive pulmonary disease (COPD).

recreational therapy: A specialized type of therapy that uses recreation—such as games, sports, crafts, dance, music, work with animals, and more—to help people with illnesses or disabilities recover, maintain well-being, or lead a fuller and healthier life.

rehabilitation: The process of returning someone to a healthier state, better health, or a more functional life after an illness or accident.

SAT: One of the standardized tests in the United States that anyone applying to undergraduate studies should take. It measures verbal and mathematical reasoning abilities as they relate to predicting successful performance in college. It is intended to complement a student's GPA and school record in assessing readiness for college. The total score of the SAT is 1600. *See also* ACT.

scholarships: Merit-based aid used to pay for postsecondary education that does not have to be paid back. Scholarships are typically awarded based on academic excellence or some other special talent, such as music or art.

Notes

Introduction

1. Bureau of Labor Statistics, United States Department of Labor, "Healthcare Occupations," www.bls.gov/ooh/healthcare/home.htm (accessed March 2, 2018).

Chapter 1

1. American Physical Therapy Association, "About Physical Therapy," policy .apta.org/about (accessed February 8, 2018).

2. Bureau of Labor Statistics, US Department of Labor, "Physical Therapists Work Environment," www.bls.gov/ooh/healthcare/physical-therapists.htm#tab-3 (accessed March 5, 2018).

3. Bureau of Labor Statistics, US Department of Labor, "Physical Therapists," www.bls.gov/ooh/healthcare/physical-therapists.htm (accessed March 5, 2018).

4. American Physical Therapy Association, "APTA History," www.apta.org/history (accessed February 9, 2018).

5. Ibid.

6. Adapted from Bureau of Labor Statistics, US Department of Labor, "Physical Therapists."

7. American Occupational Therapy Association, "What Is Occupational Therapy?," www.aota.org/Conference-Events/OTMonth/what-is-OT.aspx (accessed February 10, 2018).

8. Ibid.

9. Ibid.

10. All Allied Health Schools, "How to Become an Occupational Therapist," www.allalliedhealthschools.com/physical-therapy/how-to-become-occupational-therapist (accessed February 11, 2018).

11. Adapted from Bureau of Labor Statistics, US Department of Labor, "Occupational Therapists," www.bls.gov/ooh/healthcare/occupational-therapists.htm (accessed March 2, 2018).

12. National Council for Therapeutic Recreation Certification, "About Recreational Therapy," nctrc.org/about-ncrtc/about-recreational-therapy (accessed March 4, 2018).

13. Bureau of Labor Statistics, US Department of Labor, "Recreational Therapists," www.bls.gov/ooh/healthcare/recreational-therapists.htm (accessed February 11, 2018).

14. Adapted from https://www.bls.gov/ooh/healthcare/recreational-therapists.htm.

15. HealthTimes, "What Is an Exercise Physiologist?" healthtimes.com.au/hub/exercise-physiology/13/guidance/nc1/what-is-an-exercise-physiologist/577 (accessed February 11, 2018).

16. ExploreHealthCareers.org, "Exercise Physiologist," explorehealthcareers.org/career/sports-medicine/exercise-physiologist (accessed February 10, 2018).

17. American Society of Exercise Physiologists, "Accreditation," www.asep.org/professional-services/accreditation (accessed February 11, 2018).

18. Adapted from https://www.bls.gov/ooh/healthcare/exercise-physiologists.htm.

19. Bureau of Labor Statistics, US Department of Labor, "What Massage Therapists Do," www.bls.gov/ooh/healthcare/massage-therapists.htm#tab-2 (accessed February 11, 2018).

20. Adapted from Bureau of Labor Statistics, US Department of Labor, "Massage Therapists," www.bls.gov/ooh/healthcare/massage-therapists.htm (accessed March 2, 2018).

21. Natural Healers, "History of Massage Therapy," www.naturalhealers.com/massage-therapy/history (accessed February 20, 2018).

22. Bureau of Labor Statistics, US Department of Labor, "How to Become an Athletic Trainer," www.bls.gov/ooh/healthcare/athletic-trainers.htm#tab-4 (accessed February 13, 2018).

23. HealthCare Careers, "Athletic Trainer," www.healthcarecareers.org/athletic-trainer (accessed February 13, 2018).

24. Adapted from Bureau of Labor Statistics, US Department of Labor, "Athletic Trainers," www.bls.gov/ooh/healthcare/athletic-trainers.htm (accessed March 2, 2018).

Chapter 2

1. OT Plan, "How to Obtain Your Occupational Therapy Degree," www.otplan.com/articles/how-to-obtain-your-occupational-therapy-degree.aspx (accessed December 18, 2017).

2. "COE Guidelines for an Occupational Therapy Fieldwork Experience—Level II," https://www.aota.org/-/media/corporate/files/educationcareers/educators/fieldwork/levelii/coe%20guidelines%20for%20an%20occupational%20therapy%20fieldwork%20experience%20--%20level%20ii--final.pdf (accessed December 18, 2017).

3. Study.com, "Therapeutic Recreation Specialist Certification Information," study.com/recreation_therapy_degrees.html (accessed December 18, 2017).

4. Learn.org, "Therapeutic Recreation Master's Degree Programs," learn.org/articles/Therapeutic_Recreation_Masters_Degree_Program_FAQs.html (accessed December 18, 2017).

5. Study.com, "Recreation Therapist: Job Description, Duties and Requirements," study.com/articles/Recreation_Therapist_Job_Description_Duties_and_Requirements.html (accessed December 18, 2017).

6. Exercise Science Guide, "Exercise Physiologist: Overview," www.exercise-science-guide.com/careers/exercise-physiologist (accessed December 19, 2017).

7. National Athletic Trainers' Association, "Degree Change FAQs," www.nata.org/career-education/education/resources-tools/degree-change-faqs (accessed December 19, 2017).

8. National Athletic Trainers' Association, "Education Overview," www.nata.org/about/athletic-training/education-overview (accessed December 19, 2017).

9. LinkIn.com, "New Survey Reveals 85% of All Jobs Are Filled Via Networking," www.linkedin.com/pulse/new-survey-reveals-85-all-jobs-filled-via-networking-lou-adler(accessed December 19, 2017).

10. NewGradPhysicalTherapy.com, "Leverage Your Volunteering Experience When Applying to Physical Therapy School," newgradphysicaltherapy.com/volunteer-experience-physical-therapy-school (accessed December 20, 2017).

11. American Occupational Therapy Association "Level II Fieldwork," www.aota.org/Education-Careers/Fieldwork/LevelII.aspx (accessed December 21, 2017).

Chapter 3

1. *U.S. News & World Report*, "Finding a Good College Fit," June 13, 2011, www.usnews.com/education/blogs/the-college-admissions-insider/2011/06/13/finding-a-good-college-fit (accessed January 21, 2018).

2. National Center for Education Statistics, "Fast Facts: Graduation Rates," nces.ed.gov/fastfacts/display.asp?id=40 (accessed January 21, 2018).

3. US Department of Education, "Focusing Higher Education on Student Success," July 27, 2015, www.ed.gov/news/press-releases/fact-sheet-focusing-higher-education-student-success (accessed January 21, 2018).

4. The Balance, "Careers in Allied Health Care," February 9, 2018, www.thebal ance.com/careers-in-allied-health-care-525853 (accessed February 19, 2018).

5. Gap Year Association, "Gap Year Data & Benefits," gapyearassociation.org/ data-benefits.php (accessed February 20, 2018).

6. Bureau of Labor Statistics, US Department of Labor, "Healthcare Occupations," www.bls.gov/ooh/healthcare (accessed February 20, 2018).

7. *U.S. News & World Report,* "Best Physical Therapy Programs," 2016, www.us news.com/best-graduate-schools/top-health-schools/physical-therapy-rankings (accessed February 20, 2018).

8. Best Medical Degrees, "30 Most Affordable Doctor of Physical Therapy (DPT) Degrees," February 21, 2007, www.bestmedicaldegrees.com/cheapest-physical -therapy-doctorate-degrees (accessed February 20, 2018).

9. Bureau of Labor Statistics, US Department of Labor, "Occupational Therapists," www.bls.gov/ooh/healthcare/occupational-therapists.htm (accessed February 20, 2018).

10. *U.S. News & World Report,* "Best Occupational Therapy Programs," 2016, www .usnews.com/best-graduate-schools/top-health-schools/occupational-therapy-rankings (accessed February 20, 2018).

11. Bureau of Labor Statistics, US Department of Labor, "Recreational Therapists," www.bls.gov/ooh/healthcare/recreational-therapists.htm (accessed February 20, 2018).

12. Schoolchoices.org, "Recreational Therapy," www.schoolchoices.org/colleges/ major/774 (accessed April 12, 2018).

13. Bureau of Labor Statistics, US Department of Labor, "Exercise Physiologists," www.bls.gov/ooh/healthcare/exercise-physiologists.htm (accessed February 20, 2018).

14. Study.com, "Top Schools with Exercise Science & Exercise Physiology Programs," https://study.com/articles/Top_Exercise_Science_and_Exercise_Physiology _Programs_List_of_Top_Schools.html (accessed May 10, 2018).

15. CollegeCalc, "Cheapest Colleges for Kinesiology and Exercise Science," www.collegecalc.org/majors/kinesiology-and-exercise-science (accessed February 20, 2018).

16. Bureau of Labor Statistics, US Department of Labor, "Athletic Trainers," www.bls.gov/ooh/healthcare/athletic-trainers.htm (accessed February 20, 2018).

17. Monster.com, "Best Athletic Training Degrees and Colleges," www.monster .com/career-advice/article/5-colleges-for-athletic-trainer-majors (accessed February 21, 2018).

18. American Massage Therapy Association, "Starting a Career in Massage Therapy," www.amtamassage.org/professional_development/starting.html (accessed February 22, 2018).

19. Federation of State Massage Therapy Boards, "Massage & Bodywork Licensing Examination," www.fsmtb.org/mblex (accessed February 22, 2018).

20. Bureau of Labor Statistics, US Department of Labor, "Massage Therapists," www.bls.gov/ooh/healthcare/massage-therapists.htm (accessed February 20, 2018).

21. Federal Student Aid, US Department of Education, "FAFSA Changes for 2017–2018," studentaid.ed.gov/sa/about/announcements/fafsa-changes (accessed February 27, 2018).

Chapter 4

1. Justin Ross Muchnick, *Teens' Guide to College & Career Planning*, 12th ed. (Lawrenceville, NJ: Peterson's, 2015), 179–80.

2. Mind Tools, "Active Listening: Hear What People Are Really Saying," www .mindtools.com/CommSkll/ActiveListening.htm (accessed March 5, 2018).

Resources

*A*re you looking for more information about a particular healthcare/fitness field or even about a branch within a field? Do you want to know more about the college application process or need some help finding the right educational fit for you? Do you want a quick way to search for a good college or school? Try these resources as a starting point on your journey toward finding a great career!

Books

Fiske, Edward. *Fiske Guide to Colleges.* Naperville, IL: Sourcebooks, 2018.

Gresham, Barbara B. *Today's Health Professions: Working Together to Provide Quality Care.* Philadelphia: F. A. Davis, 2016.

Muchnick, Justin Ross. *Teens' Guide to College & Career Planning,* 12th ed. Lawrenceville, NJ: Peterson's, 2015.

Muller, Arlene. *How to Survive and Maybe Even Love Health Professions School.* Philadelphia: F. A. Davis, 2017.

Princeton Review. *The Best 382 Colleges, 2018 Edition: Everything You Need to Make the Right College Choice.* New York: Princeton Review, 2018.

Websites

Accrediting Bureau of Health Education Schools
www.abhes.org
This accrediting agency is recognized by the US Department of Education and the Council for Higher Education Accreditation. The website includes a list of accredited institutions and programs, a calendar of upcoming events, a special tab for students, a section on recent publications, and much more.

American Gap Year Association
www.gapyearassociation.org
The American Gap Year Association's mission is "making transformative gap years an accessible option for all high school graduates." A gap year is a year taken between high school and college to travel, teach, work, volunteer, generally mature, and otherwise experience the world. The website has lots of advice and resources for anyone considering taking a gap year.

American Massage Therapy Association (AMTA)
www.amtamassage.org
The AMTA site offers a quick way to find out more about good schools as well as current state regulations and certification requirements. It includes a job bank and a way to search for a therapist. It also includes a research link for the latest information on the health benefits of massage.

American Occupational Therapy Association (AOTA)
www.aota.org
The AOTA is the national professional association that represents the concerns of occupational therapy practitioners and students of occupational therapy, with the goal of improving the quality of occupational therapy services. On the website, you can find information about education, careers, conferences, and other events related to occupational therapy.

American Physical Therapy Association (APTA)
www.apta.org
The APTA is the national professional association for physical therapists. From this website, you can find out about state licensing agencies, find a PT in your area, learn more about what it's like to practice as a PT, and more.

Association of Schools of Allied Health Professions
www.asahp.org
This not-for-profit professional association's members include administrators, educators, and others who are concerned with issues that affect allied health education. The website includes information about membership, upcoming conferences, ongoing educational opportunities, a newsfeed with recent updates in the field, and more.

The Balance
www.thebalance.com
This site is all about managing money and finances, but also has a large section called Your Career, which provides advice for writing résumés and cover letters, interviewing, and more. Search the site for teens and you can find teen-specific advice and tips.

Clinical Exercise Physiology Association (CEPA)
www.acsm-cepa.org
The focus of CEPA as a national organization is to advance the profession of clinical exercise physiology through advocacy, education, and career development. This site includes links to member resources, student resources, ways to network with other exercise physiologists, and a link to the organization's clinical research journal.

The College Entrance Examination Board
www.collegeboard.org
The College Entrance Examination Board tracks and summarizes financial data from colleges and universities all over the United States. This great, well-organized site can be your one-stop shop for all things college research. It contains lots of advice and information about taking and doing well on the SAT and ACT, many articles on college planning, a robust college search feature, a scholarship search feature, and a major and career search area. You can type your career of interest (for example, occupational therapy) into the search box and get back a full page that describes the career; gives advice on how to prepare, where to get experience, and how to pay for it; what characteristics you should have to excel in this career, lists of helpful classes to take while in high school, and lots of links for more information.

College Grad Career Profiles
www.collegegrad.com/careers
Although this site is primarily geared toward college graduates, the career profiles area, indicated above, has a list of links to nearly every career you could ever think of. A single click takes you to a very detailed, helpful section that describes the job in detail, explains the educational requirements, includes links

to good colleges that offer this career and to actual open jobs and internships, describes the licensing requirements (if any), lists salaries, and much more.

Commission on Accreditation of Allied Health Education Programs (CAAHEP)
www.caahep.org
CAAHEP is one of the largest program accreditors in the health sciences field. The website enables you to easily search through a large collection of accredited programs. It also includes a specific section just for students and a news and events section.

Commission on Accreditation on Athletic Training Education (CAATE)
www.caate.net
CAATE is the national organization that provides accreditation to schools and educational programs. You can use the site to search for accredited programs in good standing. The Students tab includes information about becoming an athletic trainer and a way to search programs throughout the United States.

Explore Health Careers
www.explorehealthcareers.org
As the title suggests, this site enables you to explore careers in the health fields. You can seek information to help you decide whether a career in health is right for you, find the right fit and focus your search within the many fields, actually find the job or internship you're looking for, learn more about paying for college, and more.

Federation of State Boards of Physical Therapy (FSBPT)
www.fsbpt.org
The FSBPT helps develop a strong foundation of laws and regulatory standards in physical therapy. Pretty much anything you would need to know to become and stay licensed as a PT is found on this site, including the various state requirements, how to get licensed in a different state, how to sign up for upcoming exams, how to prepare, and more.

Khan Academy

www.khanacademy.org

The Khan Academy website is an impressive collection of articles, courses, and videos about many educational topics in math, science, and the humanities. You can search any topic or subject (by subject matter and grade), and read lessons, take courses, and watch videos to learn all about it. The site includes test prep information for the SAT, ACT, AP, MCAT, GMAT, and other standardized tests. There is also a College Admissions tab with lots of good articles and information, provided in the approachable Khan style.

Live Career

www.livecareer.com

This site has an impressive number of resources directed toward teens for writing résumés and cover letters, as well as interviewing.

Mapping Your Future

www.mappingyourfuture.org

This site helps young people figure out what they want to do and maps out how to reach career goals. Includes helpful tips on résumé writing, job hunting, interviewing, and more.

Massage TherapyLicense.org

www.massagetherapylicense.org

This website contains a state-by-state listing of requirements for licensing, education, and certification of massage therapists. This site has a clickable map and alphabetical listing of states, and with a single click you can easily find any state's requirements.

Monster.com

www.monster.com

Monster.com is perhaps the most well-known and certainly one of the largest employment websites in the United States. You fill in a couple of search boxes and away you go. You can sort by job title, of course, as well as by company name, location, salary range, experience range, and much more. The site also includes information about career fairs, advice on résumés and interviewing, and more.

National Board for Certification in Occupational Therapy (NBCOT)
www.nbcot.org
The NBCOT website has all the information you'll need to get and stay certified as an occupational therapist, including a portal to state regulatory bodies.

National Council for Therapeutic Recreation Certification (NCTRC)
www.nctrc.org
NCTRC is an international organization dedicated to professional excellence through the certification of recreational therapists. NCTRC grants the Certified Therapeutic Recreation Specialist (CTRS) credential, which is offered to qualified individuals based on stringent requirements.

Occupational Outlook Handbook
www.bls.gov
The US Bureau of Labor Statistics produces this website, which offers lots of relevant and updated information about various careers, including average salaries, how to work in the industry, job market outlook, typical work environments, and what workers do on the job. See www.bls.gov/emp/ for a full list of employment projections.

Peterson's College Prep
www.petersons.com
In addition to lots of information about preparing for the ACT and SAT and easily searchable information about scholarships nationwide, the Peterson's site includes a comprehensive search feature for universities and schools based on location, major, name, and more.

Study.com
www.study.com
Similar to Khan Academy, Study.com allows you to search any topic or subject and read lessons, take courses, and watch videos to learn all about it. The site includes a good collection of information about the allied health professions.

TeenLife
www.teenlife.com
This site calls itself "the leading source for college preparation" and includes lots of information about summer programs, gap year programs, community service, and more. Promoting the belief that spending time out "in the world" outside of the classroom can help students develop important life skills, this site contains lots of links to volunteer and summer programs.

U.S. News & World Report *College Rankings*
www.usnews.com/best-colleges
U.S. News & World Report provides almost fifty different types of numerical rankings and lists of colleges throughout the United States to help students with their college search. You can search colleges by best reviewed, best value for the money, best liberal arts schools, best schools for B students, and more.

About the Author

Kezia Endsley is an editor and author from Indianapolis, Indiana. In addition to editing technical publications and writing books for teens, she enjoys running and triathlons, traveling, reading, and spending time with her family and seven pets.

EDITORIAL BOARD